Dedication

This book is dedicated to my loving wife, Nicole, and my adorable daughter, Baleigh.

To Nicole, my Booty Bear.

You have been my number one fan since the day we met. You have always been in my corner, through thick and thin. I could not have asked for a more loving, more caring, and more supportive wife than you. We are where we are today because we make the most amazing team. You have made life worth living on so many levels. I could not imagine being on this journey without you. You are my rock, my pillar of stability, and my bestie for my restie! I love you more today, than I did yesterday, but not as much as I will tomorrow. Thank you for loving me.

To Baleigh, my little Tortilla Gorilla!

You have made me so proud. I'll never forget the night mommy and I brought you home from the hospital and I held you in my arms while lying in bed in the middle of the night. I remember looking into your eyes, and for a split second, as you looked back, I felt as if you looked right into my soul. It took my breath away and my heart overflowed with so much joy and happiness. I knew right then in there, that you were very, very special. You've done such amazing things in your life. I've enjoyed watching your art evolve over time, your writing and storytelling skills grow, and how much you've developed into a beautiful, polite, caring and loving, young lady. I love you with all my heart. Remember that always!

About the author

Chris Burfield is the CEO and Founder of VanBurf Media, a Digital Marketing Agency that helps business owners and entrepreneurs generate more leads and sell more products and services through social media and other online platforms. He was born in Robinson, Pennsylvania. His father was a coal miner, later turned Methodist Minister while his mother was a stay-at-home mom. They lived in a double wide trailer on the outskirts of town.

Chris learned a strong work ethic at a very young age and says this has played a key role in his success. As a young child, he began his entrepreneurial career in first grade by drawing pictures of popular Sunday Newspaper Comics and selling them to kids in his class for $0.10 each. In his early teens, he earned money by starting a lawn-mowing business, snow-shoveling service and newspaper route. At age 17, Chris became a dishwasher at a local steak and seafood restaurant, making just $4.30/ hour. It was at this time in his life that he discovered that working for other people was not what he wanted to do the rest of his life.

Fast forward to 1994, he went off to college with an undecided major, but by his second year, decided he would major in Sociology. In 1996, he failed out of college, and after working several jobs, finally ended up working in a Chiropractic office as a Chiropractic Assistant. It was here he would find purpose in his life. In 2000, Chris moved to Dallas, Texas to pursue a career as a Chiropractor, but would end up failing out of college a second time. But didn't let that interfere with his goals to become a self-made man.

Although he never became a Chiropractor himself, in 2003, he opened a Chiropractic office of his own with a business partner who was a Chiropractor. Within 7 years, Chris built that office into one of the most successful practices in the state of Texas through strategic marketing. In 2010, Chris sold his half of the practice to his business partner to pursue the next chapter in his life of teaching online marketing strategies.

Chris rose to prominence in 2010 after establishing himself as one the foremost experts in marketing within the Chiropractic profession, and in 2015, established VanBurf Media, a Digital Marketing Agency that helps business owners and entrepreneurs generate more leads and sell more products and services. Chris is currently the host of Propaganda Marketing Machine, an online show highlighting strategic marketing strategies that can catapult your business to the next level.

Table of Contents

Chapter 1
Propaganda Marketing Machine

"The best marketing doesn't feel like marketing."
-Tom Fishburne

I want to help you create an insanely loyal following. I want to help you make your ideas stick. I want to help you achieve the freedom you desire.

This book is designed to help you build your own propaganda marketing machine via online marketing with social media platforms like YouTube, Google, Instagram, Facebook, and Twitter. With this book, business owners and entrepreneurs will learn how to best take advantage of these rapidly growing online platforms.

If you're not currently a business owner or an entrepreneur, don't put this book down yet! Some of you reading this right now may be working a nine to five job that you absolutely hate. Those types of jobs don't make life fun. If that's you and you're looking to find a way to escape, starting your own business might be something worth considering. My advice will be invaluable for you, too.

I got my start in online marketing back in 2006. At that time, I was an equal equity partner in a chiropractic office with a good friend of mine. We were growing the business together, but it got to a point where we started really butting heads on a lot of things. He wanted to take things in one direction while I felt another direction would be better for the business.

Our conflict and constant disagreements became very stressful and frustrating! My health even started to decline as a result of the tension produced from working in this type of environment. I thought to myself, *"You know, I wonder if there's a way I can maybe make money online?"*

My ultimate goal was to start an online business and make enough money that I would be put in a position of power. With enough stable income, I could either walk away from the toxic partnership with my business partner or possibly interest him in a buyout. I dreamed of the day when I could go to him and say, *"Hey look: I really don't need you, this business, or this business partnership anymore. Let's do a buyout."*

But let's rewind a bit, first. Let's cover the history of the partnership. That will lead us to how I saw my first opportunity for online marketing.

I'm not a chiropractor myself, but I have spent over 20 years in the chiropractic profession. During the first six years of my career, I was a chiropractic assistant. In 2002, a good friend of mine (at that time) was graduating from chiropractic school. He said to me, *"Hey, I know that you're doing a lot of work in chiropractic offices right now. I know part of your job includes carrying out spinal screenings, giving corporate health talks, engaging in internal marketing promotions, teacher appreciation events, referral programs, and networking with medical doctors to get patients."* He thought we both might benefit from a partnership in which I handled the marketing while he cared for patients. He proposed a 50/50 partnership and I agreed to it. We ran the business together for seven years. Two years into the partnership, though, I wanted out.

At the end of 2005, I was looking for some waiting room DVDs for our chiropractic office, so I decided to look on ebay. It's common for chiropractic offices to have a big screen TV in their office in which they play patient education DVDs consisting of slideshows with a variety of health topics. The point of the DVDs is to inform people about health, wellness, and the role chiropractic played in that. Anyway, I found a company selling them, but they were charging $100 for one DVD or you could buy a set of 12 for $1,000. There was no way in hell I was going to pay that much money for one DVD, let alone buy 12 at that price. As I looked at the samples they had I thought, *"I wonder if I could create my own DVDs?*

So I went to work! Over the next few weeks, I created my first DVD. It was 60 minutes long and I have to admit, it was pretty awesome! Patients loved it. My mind naturally moved one step ahead and I thought to myself, *"I wonder if I could sell this on eBay?"* It didn't take me long to find out. I posted my own waiting room DVD on eBay and within a few minutes, someone opted to "Buy It Now" for $25. I was astonished, thinking, *"Holy crap! Someone actually bought that thing."*

After my first sale, I went ahead and listed another one quickly. In about 15 minutes, I got a notification that I had sold another DVD. I was so marveled that I ended up listing three DVDs at the same time. By the end of the day, I had sold all three of them. I realized that I had actually created something that people really wanted and were looking for - and I could make some real dough selling it!

Naturally, I continued selling my DVDs. In my first month, I made $1,000 on eBay by selling the DVDs for $25 apiece. Since the DVDs costed about $5 apiece to make, I was making $20 profit per DVD. Encouraged by my success and driven forward by my entrepreneurial mind, I thought, *"Well, what if I make 2, 3, 4, 5, or maybe even 6 different DVDs and I have an entire series?"* I purchased a program called *Print Shop* from Office Depot for $49, started putting together images and slides accompanied by text, and worked hard to make my vision of creating an entire series a reality.

I came up with this whole series of DVDs, called TIC Talk (TIC standing for ChiropracTIC). By the end of the year, I had created eight DVDs and gave the series a price tag of $397. I knew I needed a website, so I hired a web developer to build one for me. I actually went through two different websites before building my own. The first two website developers totally screwed me. They created two piece of shit websites that looked nothing like I envisioned. So I built my own website by watching some tutorials on YouTube. I made a big mistake, though: I didn't know the first thing about online marketing.

I thought just having a website was enough. I honestly thought that people were just going to find it online and buy my stuff. I thought this was going to be easy peasy and that I was going to make all this money. Unfortunately, I had to learn the hard way that simply building a website and putting it up doesn't necessarily generate sales. It only generates sales if people know about the website. I was missing an essential step: driving traffic.

Luckily for me, I had an email list that consisted of hundreds of emails. Back in the day, eBay used to give you the email address of the person who purchased your product. From my DVD sales, I had accumulated several hundred emails which I put onto a spreadsheet. I loaded them up into an email platform called Mailloop (which doesn't even existent anymore). Man, talk about a time-consuming way to simply send emails. It wasn't like Aweber, Mailchimp, or Infusionsoft. I had to download this software to my desktop, setup the SMTP, attach it to my website hosting account, and send emails that way. It was daunting and just plain sucked. Aweber is the main platform I use now, along with Actionetics from ClickFunnels.

Anyway, I sent out an email to everybody on my list, saying *"Hey, you bought this DVD from me. I don't know if you know this or not, but I created a whole bunch of other DVDs and there's a whole series of them now. There are eight DVDs in all and the series is called TIC Talk. Here are the topics and what they discuss. This would be great for your waiting room."* I sent that email out and it wasn't long before I collected $6,000 in sales! I was blown away. I thought to myself, *"Wow! It took me 10 minutes to write that email and I made $6,000!"*

Long story short, I made $12,000 my first year selling on Ebay. The next year, when I started marketing through email, I made $24,000. The following year, I made $52,000. By my fourth year, I broke six figures online. Now, I run a seven-figure business online. So that's how I got started selling stuff online. I learned quickly that the internet can be a very powerful tool for generating lots of passive income - if you know how market properly.

Since that time, we've been introduced to social media. In my opinion, social media platforms are extremely underutilized by business owners looking to generate new clientele, new customers, new patients, and selling their products or services online. To bring my story full circle, that's the purpose of this book; I want to show you how you can use platforms like Facebook, YouTube, Instagram, and email marketing more effectively to promote your businesses. I want to show you how to build a propaganda marketing machine that distributes your content so people are seeing you everywhere, you're actually grabbing their attention, delivering vaule and making sales.

No matter what industry you're in, you want to get the attention of people that might be interested in whatever product or service you're offering or whatever business you're promoting. If you're not getting attention and you're not making it known who you are, then you are obscure. Obscurity is what kills businesses. I want to help you leave obscurity behind with this book by teaching you how to become not only visible, but prominent in your niche. I want to help you expand beyond measure. In the subsequent chapters, we're going to cover many different topics. I'm going to share a lot of ideas and strategies that you can use to help your business thrive.

There are different techniques which can be used in your business to help attract more people and ultimately make them buy whatever it is you might be selling. During the course of this book, we'll talk about some of these different techniques.

A number of people have asked me, *"Why are you using the word 'Propaganda' in your book title? Isn't propaganda a negative term?"* It's a good question, but they're mistaken. Although "propaganda" has negative connotations in many people's minds, it's not necessarily a negative term. Propaganda is majorly about public relations - being able to establish a rapport between you and your potential clientele or customers.

The godfather of propaganda and father of public relations is a guy named Edward Bernays. One thing Bernays said is that propaganda in and of itself is neutral: it's neither good nor bad. It all depends on how it is used. Propaganda is a way to influence people and spread ideas, whether you want to use it for good and spread the truth or you want to use it for evil and spread deception. It's an extremely powerful force and one to be recognized. My sincere belief is that propaganda can be used by your business in a positive way, and to great effect.

Bernays expanded on propaganda by saying, *"Truth is mighty and must prevail, and if any body of men believe that they have discovered a valuable truth, it is not merely their privilege but their duty to disseminate that truth. If they realize, as they quickly must, that this spreading of truth can be done upon a large scale and effectively only by organized effort, they will make use of the press and the platform as the best means to give it wide circulation. Propaganda becomes vicious and reprehensive only when its authors consciously and deliberately disseminate what they know to be lies, or when they aim at effects which they know to be prejudicial to the common good."*

What you do with the information in this book is up to you. I can't stop anyone from abusing it, but I sincerely hope that you won't! Quite simply, I wanted to first clarify that propaganda in and of itself is neutral. I implore you to join me by using it for good. Bernays also had this to say about propaganda, *"The only propaganda which will ever tend to weaken itself as the world becomes more sophisticated and intelligent, is propaganda that is untrue or unsocial."* You'll benefit by keeping this in mind.

Bernays is responsible for a lot of things that we believe about certain aspects of life. For example, when you think of a traditional American breakfast, bacon and eggs probably come to mind. Your unquestioned association of the American breakfast with bacon and eggs is the direct result of a campaign Bernays put together to help generate more sales for bacon. Here's the down low on that story:

"In the 1920s, Bernays was approached by the Beech-Nut Packing Company – producers of everything from pork products to the nostalgic Beech-Nut bubble gum. Beech-Nut wanted to increase consumer demand for bacon. Bernays turned to his agency's internal doctor and asked him whether a heavier breakfast might be more beneficial for the American public. Knowing which way his bread was buttered, the doctor confirmed Bernays suspicion and wrote to five thousand of his doctors friends asking them to confirm it as well. This 'study' of doctors encouraging the American public to eat a heavier breakfast – namely 'Bacon and Eggs' – was published in major newspapers and magazines of the time to great success. Beech-Nut's profits rose sharply thanks to Bernays and his team of medical professionals."

Bernays' influence stretched far beyond breakfast. During the 1920s, it was taboo for women to smoke cigarettes in public. Bernays is the man responsible for ending that taboo. He accomplished this feat by staging an event that ended up getting printed in the newspapers the next day. That single event and its resulting media coverage changed the way people thought about women smoking.

Every year, New York held an Easter day parade which was attended by thousands. Bernays decided to use this public event to his advantage. He persuaded a group of rich debutantes to hide cigarettes under their clothes and join the parade. When they were given a signal from Bernays, they were to light up the cigarettes dramatically. Bernays then informed the press that he had heard that a group of suffragettes (a women's organiza-tion during the late 19th and early 20th century) were preparing to pro-test by lighting up what they called "Torches of Freedom." Ask yourself, *"What appears on all American coins?"* It's Lady Liberty and she's holding up the torch.

Remember Sigmund Freud, the famous founder of psychoanalysis? He was Bernays' uncle. When he was a child, Bernays would sit at the dinner table and listen to conversations between his uncle, his father, and the rest of the family. Freud's genius in the field of psychology undoubt-edly rubbed off on Bernays. Bernays' symbolism of cigarettes as *"torches of freedom for women in America"* must have been inspired by good old Uncle Freud.

He knew any sort of protest at such a large event would cause com-motion and he knew that there would be no shortage of photographers there to capture the moment. The result was a powerful combination: not only women, but young women - debutantes! - smoking cigarettes in pub-lic. To top that iconic image off, the phrase "Torches of Freedom" encour-ages all supporters of equality to support women in their smoking. There's emotion, there's memory, and there's a rational phrase. It was pure genius.

If Bernays could get an entire nation to accept women smoking and if he could make bacon and eggs the standard American breakfast, then just think about what you can do with your product, service, or business by promoting it online. You can use the same techniques and strategies to actually grow a loyal following of individuals that will cry out to you, *"Hey, I want what you have! Please take my money!"*

Recently, I spoke to a young chiropractor over the phone. He went to a seminar held by a very popular figure in the chiropractic profession. At the end of his presentation, the man on stage offered his products for sale and the guy I was talking to over the phone said, *"I literally stood up and said, 'Please take my money.'"* He was a huge follower of the man and he wanted what he had. The young chiropractor continued by telling me that he has been following the chiropractic guru for years. He consumes everything the guy puts out! The loyalty comes for a deep sense of connection with his brand, personality, and products. That's where I want you and your business to get to.

I want you to get to the point where you attract a following of people that love what you do because you actually help them improve their life in some way, shape, or form. I want them to feel deeply connected to you, and as a result of that, pay you handsomely for your products or services.

By telling my story and illustrating the power of propaganda by explaining Bernays' successes, I hope I've been able to explain what this book is about and the reason for my choice of using the word "Propaganda," and the whole purpose of my efforts. Ultimately, it is to help you grow your business, make more money, become more profitable, and most importantly, help you and others experience greater freedom in life.

Like I said at the very beginning, I found myself in a stressful situation in my business. It was online marketing that allowed me to build a business where I was actually earning more money online marketing than I was in the brick and mortar style business I once had.

It has been eight years since I sold the other business and it has been the most amazing eight years of my life. I get to spend every day with my family. I work from home. I answer to no one but myself. I have low overhead. I run a very successful Facebook ad agency. Most importantly, I'm happy. It has been an amazing ride so far and I want you to join the ride. I want to help you achieve whatever goals you have and get the freedom you've always desired.

Chapter 2
Social Media- The 7 Laws of Influence (I)

"I hold that a strongly marked personality can influence descendants for generations."
-Beatrix Potter

People go into business for a variety of reasons and operate their businesses in all sorts of ways. Whether you're an entrepreneur, a business owner, an online marketer, or just starting out altogether, the bottom line is that you have something you believe in, you find value in, and you know can help other people. In order for your business to thrive, you have to sell this value proposition, whether it's in the form of a product or a service. The purpose of this book is to teach you how to do exactly that - in the most profitable possible way.

The Seven Laws of Influence are vital to achieving any sort of success in online marketing. We'll cover these laws by splitting them up into two chapters. The Seven Laws of Influence are entirely based on Robert Cialdini's excellent book, <u>Pre-Suasion</u>, which came out in September 2016.

These laws of influence have always been around; Cialdini didn't create them. He did, however, do an exceptional job in explaining how the laws of influence can be used in business and marketing for tremendous results. In the first chapter of this book, I mentioned Edward Bernays, the godfather of public relations and marketing. Bernays was actually the one who coined the term "Public Relations" from the word "Propaganda." The singular reason Bernays opted against using "Propaganda" was the Germans' bastardization of the word during the war, which resulted in "Propaganda" gaining a negative connotation. Always a man of solutions, Bernays introduced the term "Public Relations," a phrase untainted by negative history.

The first law of influence is the Law of Reciprocity. What is reciprocity? In the simplest manner of speaking, it's about me giving you something and your resulting feeling of obligation to give me something back. We've probably all experienced this at some point in our lives. An important part of reciprocity is that the obligation of giving something back is never explicitly imposed; it's a natural feeling. It's when someone does something nice for you and then you're like, *"You know what? I need to do something really nice for them, too."* It comes from within you.

Maybe someone sent you a Starbucks gift card in the mail. Or maybe they picked your kids up from school for you. It felt like a really nice, totally selfless gesture, so you went ahead and returned the favor. That's the whole idea of reciprocity. *"I'm going to give to you, just for the sake of giving to you. I'm going to give you something really cool, really valuable. I'm not going to ask for anything in return… but you'll probably feel that it's necessary to do something for me, too."*

When you use the Law of Reciprocity in business, you're ultimately hoping that by giving enough value to people, they say, *"Hey, I'm going to buy some of your stuff."* Gary Vaynerchuk, who is quite prominent amongst entrepreneurs and marketers, wrote a book called Jab, Jab, Jab, Right Hook. Vaynerchuk uses the phrase "Jab, Jab, Jab" to represent give, give, give. I'm going to give, give, give value. The "Right Hook" comes after the jabs and it's about asking for the sale.

Now that we've explained the Law of Reciprocity, you might be wondering, *"How can I actually use it?"* Here's how I use it in my business: I constantly put out valuable content - things like blog posts, YouTube videos, Instagram posts, Facebook videos - all for free. It's all free for the user to consume, but the important part is that it gives value. This content consists of ideas and strategies you can actually use and apply in your business. My aim is that no matter what it is I put out, you can apply it and get some sort of return or result in your business. For example, I used the Law of Reciprocity during my first product launch and generated over $100,000 as a result.

During this launch, I produced three content-filled videos all based around how to generate more referrals to your business. I gave all sorts of ideas, tips and strategies for attracting more customers, clients, and patients to a business or practice. What I wanted to do was to help my audience get some sort of result in advance. I wanted my free content to produce a tangible impact before I actually asked for the sale.

During the course of launching my paid product, I put out my three free videos in one week's time. Then, I had a fourth video - my sales pitch video. In that video, I said, *"If you liked the content in my previous videos, you're going to love this online course I created for you."* Here's what happened: people watched my three free videos and started applying what they had learnt to their businesses. From their application of the various ideas, tips, and strategies, they started getting more referrals. My email account was filled with people who wrote to me and said something to the tune of, *"Hey Chris, that strategy you went over in video number two was awesome. I did it this week, and I ended up with six new patients from it."* They were getting their desired results. And it's because I was actually giving away my best content and strategies.

Too many marketers and entrepreneurs try to hold back "the good stuff" in fear that people won't buy what they are offering because, well, they already have the good stuff. But here's what giving away your best stuff does psychologically for people: it gets them to think, *"Wow, if he gave that stuff away for free and these are the results that I got from it, I can't even imagine what must be in the paid content and the results I'll get from that. I've got to buy this product."*

In 2010, when I did my very first product launch, I generated over $100,000 from it. Why? I gave people valuable content for free. Then, when it came time for me to make a sales pitch, not only did they say, *"Wow, this stuff is awesome and it works,"* but they also felt obliged to give back, because I had given them some strategies that brought about real income for them.

One guy was able to generate $20,000 of income from implementing just one strategy from my free videos. He made twenty-grand and I was selling a product that was $597. So when I made that sales pitch, $597 seemed like a small favor from him to me in return for the $20,000 he made. That's the Law of Reciprocity. What you want to do is put out valuable content - give, give, give - then ask for a sale. You don't want to be selling stuff all the time; people get turned off from that.

If all I did was pitch my services to you, you wouldn't want to read this book. You might get through the first chapter, but you wouldn't want to read the subsequent chapters. Instead, I'm just going to keep giving you value-driven content. Then, at some point in the future - maybe if I have something to sell - you might buy it. Or maybe not. But I'm going to keep doing what I know works - and that is the Law of Reciprocity.

The next law is the Law of Likeability. Social media and the advancement of the Internet are controversial; some people argue that these things have actually devalued the human experience. They say that we don't spend as much time interacting with one another on a one-to-one basis because our attention is focused on these little devices we have called iPhones, Droids, laptops, and iPads.

Despite their argument, they haven't been able to debunk the fact that you can actually build a relationship with somebody online - and you can do it really easily without having to actually meet them face-to-face. The technological age brought us an absolutely phenomenal way to get people to know, like, and trust us. What we're talking about here is the Law of Likeability. If people like you, they will probably buy the products you're selling. For example, another marketer I'm great friends with is named Matthew Loop. Matthew has some amazing social media content that can help people build their businesses online.

I first came to know of Matt back in 2006. We both started producing chiropractic videos and uploading them to YouTube. I would title my videos with keywords like "Chiropractic Marketing, Get More New Patients," or whatever I thought chiropractors might be searching for. At that point in time, Matt and I were one of the only two people in the whole chiropractic profession that were actually making videos and posting them on YouTube.

Since we were the only people in the chiropractic niche on YouTube, when I would type in search keywords to see where my videos were ranked, of course I found Matt's videos. When Matt was doing his searches and checking his video rankings, he was seeing my videos, too. As a result, Matt and I met in person for the very first time in 2012. When we walked up to each other, he stuck out his hand and it felt as though we had known each other our whole lives. Matt said, *"Dude, I feel like I know you already."* I said, *"Man, I feel the exact same way. I've seen so many videos of you. I feel like I know you."* Because we had been watching each other's videos for years, we had this pre-existing connection with each other. We had gotten to know, like, and trust each other through online videos.

Since then, I've built relationships with all kinds of people through video. I receive messages all the time from people through email, messages, or Facebook saying, *"Hey Chris, I love your stuff and have been a big follower for a long time. I love everything you do and what you're doing for entrepreneurs."* I receive these messages because people feel like they have gotten to know, like, and trust me through my online videos.

With the advent of social media, as well, I have been able to interact and engage with people I never could have previously made contact with. I'm interacting and engaging with people everyday. If somebody posts a picture of them and their family, I'll write something like, *"Man, I love this! What great looking family!"* They might reply back with something like, *"Thank you! I love them to pieces!"* Through this type of interaction, we're able to build relationships with people and get them to actually like us. I think that's where a lot of business owners and entrepreneurs fall off: they don't engage with their audience enough.

The reality is: if you want people to really know, like, and trust you, you need to start engaging with your audience. When somebody leaves a comment under one of your videos or under a post that you made, reply to their comment and start a conversation with them.

After being likeable, the next thing you need to focus on is The Law of Social Proof. There's no better way for people to have trust in what you are offering than for them to read online reviews and see what other people are saying about your product, service, or business. With social media, customer service is more important than ever. If you don't take care of people - or worse, you try to screw them over - they are definitely going to blast it all over the internet. Getting blasted in a negative way over the internet is definitely not good public relations for your business in any way.

Customers who have been treated badly will often write horrible reviews on Google or Facebook, causing major damage to your brand. I've seen people with so much rage against brands that they even make video reviews and run Facebook ads for their videos. They would stop at nothing to make sure everybody in the community saw heard about their negative experiences.

Social proofing your business goes a long way in determining whether or not your online efforts are effective. Taking care of your customers is vital to having a profitable business. You want to take care of your customers so well that they fall in love with you and your brand. You want them to be so happy that they record a positive video testimonial for you or write an amazing review.

You can actually use social proof as a way to sell more by sending an email out to your database or running a Facebook Ad for a product or service that you're offering. You can say, *"Oh, by the way, here's what other people are saying about this product or service."* Also, to bring the reviews directly to your customers, you could go over to your Facebook reviews or Google reviews and screen-capture a picture of four or five of those reviews, insert that image in the email, and send it off. It gives your customers reassurance by showing them not just your words, but more importantly, the words of others.

In his book <u>Pre-Suasion</u>, Cialdini talks about how he and a group of people were marketing their lawn-care company's services to a community of people. They sent out direct mail pieces to the homes in the community. In this communication, they introduced themselves, the services they provided, and the costs. One of those direct mail pieces contained the verbiage, *"All your neighbors are doing it."* Those extra words gave their services an element of social proof. That ingenious verbiage and the resulting social proof brought about a significant increase in the amount of people who decided to employ the services of the lawn care company. In fact, they experienced an increase of almost 200% from their initial conversion rate. That's the power of social proof.

Recently, I had some plumbing issues. I went online and typed in, "Plumber, McKinney, Texas." I read all the reviews of all the plumbers and looked to see what their individual ratings were, too. Did they have a five-star rating, a four-star rating, a two-star rating? Of course, I chose the plumber that had the best reviews. If you're a chiropractor, what kind of reviews do people find when they search for your practice online? What others say about you dramatically affects your ability to build your practice.

If I was to search for a chiropractor, I would type, "Chiropractor, McKinney, Texas." If I came across a chiropractor who had 58 reviews and a 4.8 star rating and another who had a five-star rating but only three reviews, I would most likely choose the one with the 4.8 star rating. I would pick the person who had the most reviews - as long as he or she still had a good track record. More reviews equals more social proof, provided the reviews are mostly positive.

Of course, if you have a ton of reviews, but they're mostly negative, your social proof needs some work. I'm not going to go to somebody who has 54 reviews with a two-star rating. I'll probably go to the guy that has less reviews but a better rating instead. The exact formula is tough to nail down, but you need to understand that both quantity and quality of reviews are important.

Word of mouth is extremely valuable. If your business inspires happy customers to tell others by writing positive reviews, testimonials, or even video reviews about how amazing your product or service is, you're in great shape.

We're going to discuss Facebook ads in the fourth chapter. At the risk of being a bit premature, however, we'll touch on Facebook ads now for just a minute, because they present the opportunity for a great example of social proof. Say I'm a car salesman and I sell somebody a car. If my customer is absolutely thrilled with the service that I provided, I could ask them, *"Hey, would you mind if we did a quick video here? If we could let people know how pleased you were with the service you got here today, it would really help me out."*

If the customer agreed, I could get in the video with the customer and say *"Hey, my name is Chris Burfield, and I work for Toyota of Plano. This is Mary. We just put her in a preowned car today. It's like brand new. Mary, would you tell everybody what your experience was here today?"* Then, I would let Mary speak. Hopefully, she would tell everybody, *"Oh, it was amazing. You guys took such great care of me! You served me cappuccinos and answered all my questions. It was a pleasant experience. I was in and out. You guys didn't jack me around."* With this video, I could put out a killer Facebook ad.

If I spent just $100, targeted people in a 10 mile radius around my business, and ran that video testimonial in the newsfeed where people could see it, I could get 10,000 people to see that video (video view ads are about a penny per view). Those people who say my video would see some amazing social proof. Their positive exposure to me might influence them to seek me out if they were interested in buying a car. The result would inevitably be more sales for me.

So far, we have discussed the Law of Reciprocity, the Law of Likeability, and the Law of Social Proof. These three laws are hugely important, and even just using them will help your business immeasurably. In the next chapter, though, we'll discuss the Laws of Authority, Scarcity, Consistency, and Pre-suasion. By the end of the next chapter, you'll have a solid grasp on The Seven Laws of Influence.

Chapter 3
Social Media- The 7 Laws of Influence (II)

"Whoever controls the media, the images, controls the culture."
-Allen Ginsberg

The goal of introducing you to the Laws of Influence, which we began discussing in the previous chapter, is to help you understand human behavior. If you want to help a wide range of people with your product or service, you need to understand them. Of course, helping yourself along the way - to achieve a level of freedom that most people only dream of, perhaps - would be nice, too.

In this chapter, we're going to cover the next three Laws of Influence - the Laws Authority, Scarcity, Consistency, and Pre-Suasion. We'll also discuss how these laws can be applied in any business to help influence people while remaining ethical. Once again, I would like to emphasize that the strategies we discuss here are not to be abused. Instead, they should be used in a totally ethical way. Using these laws ethically can help you sell more products and services to people that you believe can benefit from them.

The fourth law of influence is the Law of Authority. This powerful law is about how you position yourself as an authority in your niche. In my opinion, there's no better way to express your authority than with online videos. Online videos give you an excellent opportunity to position yourself and create the perception of being an authority figure on a particular topic.

Too many people get hung up on their thoughts. They overanalyze everything and it paralyses their businesses. It causes them to fail to take that first step of action. I once heard someone say, *"I like to bake cakes. I'm a pretty good cake maker. I can make some really nice cake combinations and I have people that compliment me all the time on the cakes that I make. But I'm not really an expert at it."* Actually, you don't need to be the expert of all experts or the authority of all authorities on your topic; all you really need to know is just a little bit more than the person that doesn't know anything at all.

For example, if you made a video on how to bake a cake and Chef Gordon Ramsey watched it, he might say, *"Wow, this person has no idea what they're doing."* Ramsey is, in many people's eyes, the ultimate expert. The problem with this, though, is that there's only one Gordon Ramsey. If I needed to bake a carrot cake, I might do a YouTube search to help me along. Perhaps, I would come across your video, in which you walked me through baking a carrot cake. Then, I would make the cake, serve it to people, and enjoy their praise for my wonderful cake. Since your video helped me so much, I would see you as an authority figure. I would probably go back to watch other videos of you making other things.

In this example, you earned your authority in my eyes because your video taught me how to do something that I didn't previously know how to do. You can apply this method of gaining authority in any niche. Of course, with my 20 years of experience in the chiropractic industry, I'm most comfortable using chiropractic terms and examples. So for the next example, I'll assume the role of a chiropractor. If I wished to grow my authority in my niche, I would pick some things that I know that people want to learn about. These topics might be promoting health and wellness naturally, without the use of medication and surgeries.

With my knowledge, I could create a video about how having a positive mindset has an effect on your overall health. Another video might cover the types of exercises that can be performed to strengthen your spine and core muscles. A video explaining to people how they can detoxify themselves might really catch on. The nervous system's control over the body and nutrition's affect on health could obviously warrant videos, as well. I think you get the picture; regardless of what niche you're in, there's plenty to talk about.

After I finished my series of videos, I would create two 90 second videos giving people tips, ideas, and strategies on how to implement the things I taught them in the previous videos. I would start marketing those 90 second videos to the people in my community.

This concept can be applied to businesses of all types. If I owned a pizza place, I could sit down to make a video and say *"Hey, we make these amazing pizzas here at Big Boss Pizza and they're all homemade. In today's video, I want to show you how you can actually make one of these pizzas yourself. We've got 40 different kinds of pizza here, and today I'm going to show you how to make this one pizza we call The Bossman."*

Creating and sharing online videos builds an audience of people for you. They begin to see you as the authority figure on that topic. Most pizza places aren't teaching people how to make the pizzas they sell. Most people are not taking the time to make videos and then market those videos. They should be! The people in the interested communities often watch these videos over and over again. Creating online videos in your field of expertise gives you a huge advantage over others and positions you as an expert and authority.

The sooner you start, the better. If you jump in and start making videos right now, you can position yourself as an authority figure in a niche where maybe no one has taken the time to do such things.

As a chiropractor, using online videos to build your authority and audience could actually position you as the go-to person for chiropractic issues, and maybe more. You could suddenly become the community guru on health and wellness. How many doctors are making videos on those types of topics? How many acupuncturists? How many massage therapists? How many physical therapists? You'd be surprised. There's hardly anyone doing it. Take action by jumping in there and doing it. If you do, you could become the authority figure that everyone looks to for help and advice.

The next law of influence is the Law of Scarcity. Quite simply, things that are scarce usually appear to have more value to people than things that are abundant. To start explaining this law, I'll jump right in with an example of how you can apply it in your business. There is a cake company called Nothing Bundt Cakes where they sell nothing but Bundt cakes. Go figure.

I ended up on Nothing Bundt Cakes' email list and I think the story is worth telling. I went into their store looking to buy a Bundt cake, believe it or not. The person at the register said, *"Hey, would you like a free Bundt cake today? All you have to do is give us your email address, and we'll give you a coupon that you can redeem right now! Today!"* Giving my email address seemed like a no-brainer. The free Bundt cake in return provided instant gratification. Of course, I took them up on their offer.

Nothing Bundt Cake started sending me emails saying things like, *"Hey, for this week only, the first 500 people to stop by our store can get 50% off any Bundt cake they purchase!"* Towards the end of the week, they might send another email that said *"Hey, tomorrow is the last day that you can get these Bundt cakes at 50% off. We only have 75 spots left!"* By doing this, they created a sense of urgency and scarcity. The thought process inspired by the emails is, *"Wow, those things are normally $10 but now I can get it for $5. And there's only 75 spots left? I better get over there."* They create a sense of urgency and scarcity which caused people to rush over to their store to buy a Bundt cake.

You can use similar tactics to apply the law of scarcity in your business. Let's say you own a gym and you're running a special offer. The first 15 people to come in to the gym or call to schedule an appointment get their first month of membership for free. You could send out an initial email explaining how there are 15 spots. A few days later, you could send another email saying, *"Hey, there's only 4 spots left."* Like I mentioned earlier, ethics are important. If 15 people call you on your first day, there's no need to send any more emails about free spaces when there are none left. You don't want to lie.

I've used these strategies during my own product launches. For one launch, I ran three videos filled with content over the course of ten days. I released the first video on a Tuesday. The second video in that series went out on Thursday. The third video went out on the following Monday.

Then, I officially launched my product on Tuesday, but only allowed people to buy it for three days. If they didn't act fast enough to buy it during those three days, they were out of luck. When that three-day window elapsed at midnight on Thursday, I shut it down and the product could no longer be purchased.

During the three-day window, I sent out an email saying *"Hey, the prod-*

uct is officially available." The next day, Wednesday, another email went out, letting people know that they only had 36 hours left to get the product. On the third day, I sent several emails - early in the morning, at 3:00pm in the afternoon, and at 8:00pm at night. These emails reiterated the closing window - the scarcity. The communications were clear: *"Today is the last day," "Closing down in 12 hours,"* and *"Final Notice: Last Chance to BUY!"*

This type of scarcity really drives sales! Of course, you don't have to completely take your product off the market after your three-day window, either. After the three-day opening, the product could cost twice the amount and the availability of it may not be guaranteed outside the three-day opening. This is an example of how to use urgency and scarcity in your business.

Think long and hard about ways in which you can create scarcity in the minds of your potential customers or clients; nothing drives sales more than scarcity. And scarcity and urgency combined? That's a force to be reckoned with. I can tell you from my experience that on the first day my product became available, a few sales trickled in. 80 percent of sales came in during those last six to eight hours of that 3 day window.

I have spearheaded six-figure product launches. Even if we use the minimum of $100,000 (and I've done well beyond that with product launches), that means $80,000 in sales are coming in during the last six to eight hours. That's how powerful scarcity is. If you're not using scarcity in your business, you really need to.

The sixth law of influence is the Law of Consistency. People want to see you being consistent with what you're doing. Every day at 4:00 pm EST, people know Ellen Degeneres is coming on TV. Some of them even set their DVRs to record the show. Being consistent builds trust with your audience. Nobody wants to see a fly-by-night person. If you're not consistent, the probability is high that your sales will suffer. If you're putting out content online using social media. you should be consistent with your posts. You shouldn't go off the radar and expect your audience to still be there when you decide to come back.

I have come across business owners who have a Facebook page, but the last post they made on it was seven months ago. As an individual who is new to your brand, if I check you out on Facebook and the last post you made was seven months ago, or you just post once a month - or even once every two weeks - you lose points from me because I see that as inconsistency.

By being consistent with my marketing and branding, I'm hoping that I provide enough value to you that you'll get to know, like, and trust me. If I'm not consistent with it, you're going to tune out and I might never achieve my goals with you. Whatever it is that you're doing with your audience, make sure you remain consistent - always.

The seventh and final law of influence is the Law of Pre-suasion, which comes directly from Robert Cialdini's book, Pre-Suasion. If you haven't picked up Cialdini's book, I strongly recommend that you do. He said in his book *"That which is on the top of the mind gets acted on with strength and frequency."*

This is one of the reasons why you want to be in communication with your audience on a regular basis. You want to be visible; you want them to feel your presence always. When I first learned about Grant Cardone, I watched a few of his videos and thought to myself, *"How awesome is this guy?!"* He gets me fired up and is really entertaining. His video content always makes sense and the videos really resonated with me.

After searching Cardone out on YouTube and watching his videos, I got hooked. I binge watched every video! I went through his channel, video after video, and I wanted to find everything he had ever posted online. Then, I found out he had a podcast called *The Cardone Zone*, which I subscribed to. I went over to his Instagram page to follow him, too.

It wasn't long before I went over to his Facebook page and found out he had even more content there. I also followed him on snapchat. Aside from the fact that I was all over Grant and his posts, I discovered that he made an effort to be as visible as possible on almost every obvious platform there was. Everywhere I went, there was Grant Cardone.

Grant's presence across multiple platforms put him at the top of my mind. I recently bought one of Grant's products called *Cardone University*, which is a $5,000 product. The main reason I bought it was because it included a bonus of getting to meet him in person. I felt that having a one-on-one meeting with Cardone was worth more than the $5,000 I had paid.

On top of that, after meeting him, I paid $80K to air my show on his network. I also purchased 2 ticket to the *10X Growth Con* event at $10K a pop! I purchased the Super VIP tickets which included a cocktail party at Grant's home in Miami and a dinner party on a yacht with him and his wife Elena.

The Laws of Consistency and Pre-Suasion go hand in hand. With consistency, you can create a top-of-the-mind awareness with your audience. This type of awareness cannot be achieved by posting on your Facebook page once every couple of weeks or by making three videos a year. That type of consistency isn't going to lead to the type of freedom you desire. Instead, you need to keep putting out content so that people become familiar with your brand and you're always there at the forefront, at the top of their mind. No matter where they turn, whether it's to YouTube, Instagram, Snapchat or Facebook, you're there!

By positioning yourself as visible and staying consistent, you're helping to set the stage for products and services that you can offer later on. Again, it all comes back to Gary Vaynerchuk's *"jab, jab, jab, right hook."* You want to give, give, give. Give content, give value, and then ask for a sale. Your consistency sets the stage for that sale by "pre-suading" them and indoctrinating them into your brand.

Chapter 4
Leveraging Facebook Video Ads

"It is much easier to put existing resources to better use, than to develop resources where they do not exist."
-Anonymous

In Chapters 2 and 3, you learned The Seven Laws of Influence. In this chapter, we'll discuss how you can deploy Facebook video ads to great success. Grant Cardone once said, *"You don't want to compete, you want to dominate."* Making the most of Facebook video ads is one of the fastest ways that you can dominate your market.

Facebook video ads are cheap and devastatingly effective at getting your message out there. By creating high quality Facebook video ads and reaching a wide audience, you can become the go-to expert for your niche. And quite surprisingly, given their tremendous value, Facebook ads are one of the most underutilized methods of distributing messages.

I think the reason that Facebook video ads are so underutilized is the fact that the majority of individuals are afraid of making videos. They are afraid of what people will think. They are afraid of what they will look and sound like on video. They're afraid that people will make fun of them. These fears paralyze them and drastically hinder the growth of their businesses.

I work with a chiropractor named Joe Hudak who practices in Edison, New Jersey. Joe is not just a client of mine; over the last several years in which I've helped him market his business, we've also become great friends.

At Christmas time last year, Joe made a video which we ran as a Facebook video ad. The video got lots of attention, with hundreds of people even sharing it. It was a shockingly good value, too. That ad cost Joe just $60 and we were able to get over 48,000 people in his community to watch it. I don't know of any other form of advertising where you can spend $60 and get in front of 48,000 people in a five-day timeframe.

We knew that a lot of parents were going to be wrapping Christmas presents around the time we ran this campaign. Accordingly, Joe made a video and put some goodwill out into the community. His video discussed the implications of posture during wrapping presents. Since Joe knew many people would be wrapping with poor posture, he demonstrated correct present-wrapping posture in his video. The goal was to reach people in a fun, friendly way and also prevent some backs from being injured in the process.

Before we ran the video ad, we set our budget; for the following five days, we would spend $12 a day on the ad, totaling $60 by the end. During that five day timeframe, 48,000 people watched the video. It had hundreds of shares, dozens of comments, and hundreds of likes. To really put it in perspective, imagine this: It cost us 2/10 of a cent to get each person to watch that video on Facebook.

For Joe, his video's success positioned him in his community as a chiropractor that cared. It also got his name out there for people who never knew him as a chiropractor. They watched the video and realized *"Oh, wow! Dr. Joe Hudak is a chiropractor here in Edison, New Jersey? Great! I need a chiropractor, so I'll give him a call."* Joe ended up with scores of new patients from that video.

Prior to running the Christmas Facebook video ad, Joe and I had run various other videos together, and we continue running videos successfully. In Joe's community, no other chiropractors are posting videos. He's the only one running video ads on various topics. Presently, he's making a video on spinal decompression, showing what causes a bulging disc, how it affects people's health, and how he can help.

Joe's video ads help him stay at the top of people's minds. When they think of back problems and chiropractors, Joe is the first person that comes to mind. And since Joe is continually running ads, people think of him all the time. This is how market domination begins.

It's normally a penny per view for Facebook video ads, but shares, likes, and comments can help drive that cost down. Like I said earlier, it only cost Joe 2/10 of a penny per view. This value is amazing in contrast to some of the more traditional forms of advertising like television, billboards, and newspapers. Of course, I'm not saying those forms of media aren't effective for advertising or that you should never use them. If those forms of media are your first thoughts for reaching people, however, I urge you to keep Facebook video ads in mind.

Facebook is the biggest attention platform in the world. Over two billion people have Facebook accounts. With about 7 billion people in the world now, that means almost 33% (one third!) of the world's population is on Facebook.

While people are watching *Dancing with the Stars*, *The Bachelor*, or their favorite game shows, during commercials they go to their mobile devices to see what's going on on Facebook and other social media platforms. Hardly anyone watches commercials any more. In fact, the Super Bowl is perhaps the one special time when people care about watching commercials. And even then, there are almost certainly more people on Facebook than there are watching Super Bowl commercials.

Stop saying to yourself that you can't afford to run a Facebook ad to promote your business. Actually, you can't not afford it! It has to be a part of the running cost for your business if you're going to thrive. You have to spend some money on paid advertising to get your message out there.

Start by putting together three 90 second videos. 60-90 seconds is the sweet spot for videos on Facebook. Start producing content-filled videos based on different aspects of your niche. In chiropractic, for example, I would create videos around the top five things I enjoy teaching people about their health. Then, I would make some 60-90 second videos that provide tips and advice on how to get relief from a particular health problem.

In your videos, the point isn't to pitch your product or try to sell anything. Instead, you're creating videos to provide free value to your community. Genuinely let people know you're trying to help them. You want to start earning their trust first. You can retarget people that have watched your videos with an offer. The selling takes place in the retargeting, not the initial video. Remember: jab, jab, jab, right hook.

So, that's how you leverage Facebook Video Ads to grow your business. Even if you only have a budget of $100 for the month, you can still get your brand in front of 10,000 people for $100. The more money you have, the more people you can reach in a shorter period of time.

Chapter 5
Mistakes You're Probably Making On Social Media

"The definition of insanity is doing the same thing over and over again but expecting different result."
-Albert Einstein

I think you understand by now that social media is crucial. With it, you can reach huge numbers of people for shockingly low costs. Having a strong social media presence might be the single best thing you can do for your business. There are a number of mistakes that people make on social media, however, that can hinder their success. That's what this chapter is for. Here, we'll address some common mistakes. If you're on social media, you're probably making some of these mistakes.

One of the first mistakes I see people make on social media is the failure to complete their profiles across various platforms. If you're on Instagram, Twitter, and Facebook, you've got three profiles to fill in. Far too often, though, I see people fill them out partially or maybe even not at all! This is such a basic, simple thing that I think it just gets overlooked.

Consider this: search engines actually rank your profile. When people carry out a search through Google, Bing, or other search engines, they'll pull up your social profiles. If you're building a brand and you want people to know who you are, you need to have your profiles filled out!

One immediate benefit of completing your profile is that it lets people know that you're official. If you get big enough, there are a lot of wannabes out there that might pose as you and knock off your brand. If you go on Instagram and search out a celebrity, for example, you will probably come across their official Instagram profile and a bunch of knock off Instagram account, too. As your business grows and you get bigger and more popular, it's entirely possible that you could run into this issue, yourself. Completing your profile properly will help people find you and stop them from giving knock offs undeserved attention.

Your profile is people's first stop to find your contact details and an overview of your business. It's there to show people who you are and what you're about. In this day and age, people want to be in business with companies that align with their own personal values. Effectively communicating your essence is crucial.

In addition to filling out your profiles properly, you should have some fun with them, too. There's no reason that your information has to be boring and stereotypical, like *"graduated from XYZ School with a degree in Entrepreneurship, Creativity, and Innovation."* In fact, it's helpful if your profile is unique. People are attracted to personality.

Ideally, your profile will tell people what type of services you provide and who you are as a person, too. I do this not only with my social media, but also with my website. My website's dedicated profile area is the "About Us" page. On this page, I feature a video titled "10 Things You Didn't Know About Chris Burfield." In this video, I share some personal things about me. This is really effective at getting people more invested in not just my brand, but also me as a person.

My video, "10 Things You Didn't Know About Chris Burfield" isn't fluff; it gets really personal. Number 10 is about my Tourette syndrome. A lot of people don't know I deal with this because it's not evident when I'm talking. When I'm by myself or around my family, though, I make these little humming noises. It's not as obvious as the screaming obscenities type of Tourettes, but I make these little throat clearing noises. Anyway, it's something personal that's a bit scary to share, but it actually brings people closer to me. Don't be afraid of sharing certain details about yourself. Let your audience know you beyond just the surface!

One of the most common mistakes that's absolutely devastating is thinking that you can get visible for free. If you want to really reach a lot of people, you need to accept the fact that you have to pay to play on social media. Organic reach is nearly gone unless you have a huge following on various social media platforms. If you do have a huge following, you still need to get people to turn on their notifications for your posts. Unless you can get people to turn on their post notification, most experts estimate that your organic reach is only reaching about 5 to 7% of your audience. If you have a following of 100 people and you make a post, you're probably only going to reach 5 to 7 people organically.

On Facebook, running an ad or simply boosting it costs money. Luckily, it's currently quite cheap to run an ad. I can reach 30,000 people over the course of a month if I make a video, upload it to Facebook, and run a video ad for $10/day.

Here's the secret: your competitors are not paying to play. They're still posting their videos hoping they're going to reach their followers. They're scratching their heads and saying, *"How come nobody's seeing my stuff?"* You have to come to terms with the fact that you have to pay to play.

I have a certain amount money earmarked towards marketing each month. You should do the same; it will really move your business forward. *"But Chris,"* you say, *"my business is new and I don't have much of a budget."* If that's the case, you may have to give up the Starbucks coffees or other meaningless crap you're consuming each month. Personally, I drink Starbucks every day. I get two coffees a day, which adds up to about $120 a month. If you're doing the same thing, you can divert that money into advertising for your business. Starbucks is great, but growing your business is better. Give up the coffee or whatever it is you're indulging yourself with. You could even sell some plasma and get $60 to infuse into your marketing budget. The point is that you have to do whatever it takes. If that means making sacrifices so that you can spend money to grow your business, then you have to do that.

There's no justifiable reason for not reaching everyone who searches for you. That means being visible on every platform where people might look for you. I understand that your specific market might not be on certain platforms, but that shouldn't be a limitation. For example, I'm 42 years old and I have a Snapchat account.

Snapchat is notorious for being a young persons' platform; it used to be used exclusively by teens and millennials. Now, there's a growing market of people aged 28 to 35 that are jumping on Snapchat, so I snap daily.

Here's the point: your market might not be on a particular platform now, but who's to say they won't migrate? Years ago, Instagram was looked at as a kid's platform. Now, the fastest growing market of Instagram is 35 to 55 year old women. Things change and people are always excited about trying new social media platforms out. Every platform represents a potential goldmine of people to reach. Ignoring any single platform is a huge mistake that could really cost you a lot of business.

People think appearing on multiple social media platforms multiplies their work, but it really doesn't. You don't have to come up with a different post for every single platform. You can make small tweaks to your existing content, effectively repurposing it for different platforms. For example, when I make a video for the VanBurf Media Facebook page, I also upload it to YouTube. Then I take segments of it and put them up on Instagram. The same content can be reused and repurposed, actually cutting your workload rather than increasing it. By repurposing all of your content, you can make the most of it. Then it's everywhere. It's on YouTube, Facebook, Instagram, Snapchat and every possible platform there is.

Constantly pushing for a sale is a classic mistake that comes from the old-school of marketing. Making every post about your product or service is simply not effective on social media. People are not going to share your *"buy my stuff now"* content. Instead, remember Gary Vaynerchuk and his ideas from <u>Jab, Jab, Jab, Right Hook</u>. You need to give, give, give value-packed content.

Since 2008, I have been an ardent follower of Frank Kern, an internet marketing genius. Kern talks about giving people RIA - results in advance. Gary and Frank are basically saying the same thing. They're talking about giving to your potential customers rather than trying to take from them.

After watching your video or reading your blog most, people should be better off than they were before they engaged with your content. Your marketing should be valuable in and of itself. Everything I put out is based around the end user getting extreme value from it. If I post content, I'm doing so because I know that other business owners and entrepreneurs can really benefit from it. If I was just pitching sales all the time, people would get tired of it and they definitely wouldn't share it. You have to start providing value-driven content for whatever niche that you're in.

In an earlier chapter I gave some advice to bakers. Bakers can provide value to their community by creating baking tutorials. These videos could show people how to bake certain kinds of cakes and encourage them to give it a try for themselves. If you're effective, guess what people are going to do? They're going to share your content, helping you in your efforts toward market domination. That's how you get you engage people - with value-driven content, not constant "buy now" content.

How do you measure the ROI (return on investment) of social media? Some people think that running an ad once on Facebook and not making any sales as a result means that Facebook ads don't work. Those people are making a big mistake by looking at the wrong metrics.

I would like to paint a scenario that will help you think about metrics in a more productive and realistic way. Let's say you spend $100 on a video ad and that video gets exposed to 10,000 people in your community. Out of those 10,000 people, there are 100 people that found the video very informative because it added a lot of value to their life. Those people got something out of your post and they say, *"Hey, I like this person."* They saw that video appear in their newsfeed but they didn't take any action.

About two or three days later, you run another video ad. That video pops up in the newsfeed, and those people see it again. Now they say, *"Oh! I'm going to watch this video because the last one was really good."* They watch that video and then maybe they look to see if you have more videos.

They might go over to YouTube to do a search. If they're looking for me, for example, they might search "Chris Burfield, Propaganda Marketing Machine." They'll see a ton of other videos on my YouTube channel and begin binge watching them. The strategies, tips, and ideas they come across wow them. Then maybe they get really fired up and begin to search me out on other platforms.

After watching several videos of mine and consuming my content on different platforms, they start to wonder if I have a website where they can consume more content more directly. So they do a search and find it. Now, let's say my website offers a free mini training on "How to generate six figures through email marketing." They opt-in for that free training and get subscribed to my email list.

As a result, I end up sending them a series of emails that contain even more valuable content. In those emails, I drive them to some blog post that I wrote and they consume even more content from me. Through content across various platforms and now even email, I'm building a relationship with them. With email, I am able to communicate to them that *"Hey, I've got a webinar next week that's going to show you how you can run Facebook ads and completely dominate your niche and become the go-to expert and generate X amount of dollars from that."*

Seeing that email they say, *"I've got to be on that webinar."* So, they attend the Live Webinar Event and at the end of the webinar, I make a sales pitch and I tell them that I have product which they are going to love. In my product, I'll explain how to set up Facebook ads, dominate their market, become the go-to expert in their community, and how they can quit their nine to five job and finally experience the freedom they want in life. I tell them this product will allow them to spend more meaningful time with the people they love and care about. Then I tell them that this product normally goes for $997, but if they buy it by the end of the webinar they can get for just $397. They go ahead and click the "buy now" button and they make the purchase.

Now, all this happened six weeks after they saw my first video on social media. How am I going to measure the ROI of that? Where did the sale really come from? Was it the webinar? Was it the email I sent out that got people on the webinar? Was it my blog posts? Was it my YouTube Channel? Was it my Instagram? It had to be the webinar, right? It couldn't have been anything else, right?

To say that the sale was a result of my webinar alone and that Facebook (and everything else) had nothing to do with it wouldn't be wise or accurate. The process that led to the sale all started with a simple Facebook video ad that my customer watched. After that video, they began following me, tracking me down, hunting me down, and consuming my content over a 6 week timeframe. Eventually, they attended my webinar where they bought something from me.

It wasn't just the webinar. Really, it was everything. Eliminating any part of the process would be devastating to my business. Each component fits together like a piece of a beautiful, highly effective, highly persuasive puzzle.

Social media is a crucial element of your success, but it's not easy to measure its influence directly. You can't base it only on numbers by saying, *"I spent $100 and I made $300."* If you're new on social media platforms, know that this is where the attention is and where people are. These platforms are where you can build your brand, engineer an insanely loyal following, and generate massive income. You may not get a direct response (as in someone buying something from you immediately), but utilizing it is vital to the success of your business.

Chapter 6
Be an Expert

"An investment in knowledge pays the best interest."
-Benjamin Franklin

In this chapter, we will be focusing on being an expert without fear - even when you don't feel like you're an expert. Insecurity is a major hurdle that must be overcome if you're ever going to become a real authority in your niche. So many people approach me and say *"Hey Chris, I have an idea for an online business but I just don't feel like I'm ready. I feel like I need to study my topic more. I need learn more about it and get prepared."*

The consequence of these people's hesitancy is that they miss out on greatness. They have what's called "analysis paralysis." They have to make sure everything is in place. They want all their ducks in row. They want to know everything there is to know about their topic before they can start teaching others about it. While it's admirable and understandable, it's a huge mistake in business!

Since I started my marketing online in 2006, I've invested over $200,000 in my online education. I am constantly buying courses and learning about various topics that that I didn't know much about in the beginning. I purchased a book in 2006 called <u>The Insider Secrets to Marketing your Business Online</u> because I wanted to learn how to market my business online. That book helped me learned some strategies and tactics that really made my business grow.

While I was reading <u>The Insider Secrets to Marketing your Business Online,</u> I thought to myself, *"Man, I'd like to share some of the information with other people,"* because what I was learning was really valuable. Even though I wasn't an expert, I decided to go ahead and start sharing. Using the information from that book, I helped my best friend, Dr. Tabor Smith, create an online business. His business now generates multiple six figures per year.

I didn't know everything, but I was still able to help a friend grow a radically successful business. As a matter of fact, I hardly knew anything at all. However, I found that because I knew more than Dr. Tabor, he looked at me as an expert. I was able to share with him some of the small knowledge that I had gained and he thought I was a genius for it.

It all has to do with perception and relativity. If you know a little bit more than an individual who doesn't know anything, you're an expert in their eyes. For example, if all I know is addition and subtraction and I meet a kid in school who knows multiplication and division, that kid is a mathematical expert to me.

In the beginning, I didn't really know anything. Over time, though, I kept investing in myself and learning as I went along. To date, I still engage in constant active learning. I don't know everything about online marketing - and that's okay. I still know a lot more than most people, especially people just getting started. If you're reading this, you may be in the position I was in 12 years ago. Maybe you're new to the online world and you're totally amazed by the tips, strategies, and ideas I'm dishing out here in this book. You can be amazed, but don't be paralyzed; you don't need to know everything.

For best results, you need to get started with what you know right now by teaching it. Start teaching and attract a following. There are people out there that don't know what you know. They could benefit greatly from your knowledge. As you begin to invest in yourself, you will gain more knowledge that you can share with your audience.

In addition to gathering more knowledge in my niche, I also seek out means to learn about things as fast as I can, ideally before others do. When Facebook Live was introduced, I didn't understand the platform. Regardless, I made sure I took time to learn all there was about it. Since learning about it, I have been able to teach others how to use it effectively. They're always marveled at the things they can get done. The need to keep investing in yourself cannot be overemphasized.

There's always going to be people that know more than you, but that shouldn't discourage you from carving your own path. For example, if you want to start teaching people how to bake cakes, but you're only skilled with a couple specific types of cakes, you may not consider yourself an expert. If I watched your YouTube video and you helped me accomplish my goal of baking a carrot cake, though, you would most definitely be a guru to me. You guided me to do things I never imagined I could do.

Don't worry about what people are going to think of you. Don't worry about whether or not you're perfect. The most important thing is to get in there and start going to work. Create a blog, start making videos, send out emails, and post videos on Facebook, Instagram, and Twitter. Start putting your content out right now with just the limited knowledge that you have on the topic. If you can do that, I guarantee you're going to attract people and build a following.

Chapter 7
Domination is Immunity

"Fear less, dominate more."
-Anonymous

Why simply compete when you can dominate your market? If you're doing everything that needs to be done and whatever it takes to be successful, competition shouldn't even exist for you.

I want to share a story about my grandmother, Florence Irene Stiffey, aka Mac. Mac's nickname came from her affinity for macaroni and cheese as a little girl. Mac's lead foot is notorious and it provides a great philosophy that can be applied not only to driving, but also to dominating your market.

When I was seven years old, my grandmother started teaching me how to drive. I grew up in Pennsylvania where the back roads were perfect for our early driver's education courses. Mac kept her foot on the gas pedal and I would sit on her lap and steer. We'd only go about 10 miles.

By the time I was ten, I was actually able to drive on my own. My grandmother would take me out on those same back roads and let me drive while she sat in the passenger seat. While in the passenger's seat, my grandmother coached me by telling me when to accelerate, when to turn, when to hold the wheel steady, and when to apply the brakes.

(Since I learned to drive at such a young age, you might think I'm an awesome driver. I'm not. My wife is scared of my driving. When I drive, I see her grasp anything she can hold on to for dear life.)

One day, I was riding with my grandmother to a doctor's appointment. This time, she was totally in control of the car. I was in the passenger's seat. A young man was tailgating us. All of a sudden, he crossed the road's double yellow line, sped up alongside us, and then cut right in front of us. Did I mention that my grandmother could swear like a trucker? Mac started yelling obscenities at the driver in front of us. Then, without warning, she laid her lead foot on the gas and we shot past the young, reckless driver. We blew that guy away! I looked behind us and I couldn't even see his car. It was at that point that my grandmother turned to me and said, *"When you pass somebody, you don't pass them just to get in front of them. You blow their ass away."*

My grandmother dominated the road. That young man was no competition for her. He was left well in her dust and that's how you need to approach your market. You need to approach your market with a lead foot. Hit that gas and take off. Never look back, keep moving forward, and don't worry about what others are doing.

Focusing on your business by serving value-driven content to your followers. Genuinely help them dominate their markets and you will dominate yours. By doing so, you'll begin to position yourself as the ultimate expert and authority in your space. You'll earn celebrity status and people won't even look at other people who are doing what you're doing.

Creating content alone won't give you a foot made from lead. You have to be able to distribute that content. You've got to be able to do things that nobody else is doing and take steps that most people are not willing to take.

Success leaves clues. Take time to look at different experts and authorities in your niche. Look at what they're doing. Ask yourself "What makes them so successful?" When you figure it out, you've got somewhere to start. But you can't simply pull up alongside them and you can't just get in front of them. You've got to blow their ass away.

Chapter 8
Email Marketing 101

"Email has an ability many channels don't: creating valuable,
personal touches- at scale."
-David Newman

As a business owner utilizing social media marketing, your goal should be to get people off social media and on to your email list. Social media is indispensable for its ability help you get people's attention and build your following, but you don't have control over the platforms. Email gives you more control.

Facebook Fan and business pages were the gold standard years ago. They were self-propagating and you didn't need to pay to get your content seen by people. If you had 1,000 followers and you made a post, all 1,000 followers would see that post. Over time, Facebook switched things up. Now, getting your posts distributed to a wider audience of people requires payment. If you make that same post today with your same 1,000 followers, you'd be lucky if 5 to 7 percent of your audience saw it.

As we discussed in Chapter 5, Facebook's sudden change is not an insurmountable hurdle. However, the change required adjusting - and social media platforms can change at will. The bottom line is that they're in control. If you're relying solely on a platform that you don't own for your customer base, you're letting that platform hold your business hostage.

You can run Facebook ads and generate excellent using them, but if you want to take your marketing strategy to the next level, you need to understand the basics of email marketing.

Email marketing is a crucial component to your success. Most people are not primarily on social media to buy things; they're there to interact with their friends. The most effective way to use social media is to deliver valuable content, build a relationship with people, and eventually get them to give us their email address in exchange for some sort of content or service. Through email, we can continue providing additional value. We're still trying to build trust, create desire, and strengthen the relationship. With strong relationships, we can ultimately pitch our sales.

The first thing you need is a means of generating an email list. To achieve that, you need to provide something of value that will interest your niche. If you can get their attention and provide value, they'll give you their email addresses in exchange for it. Getting someone's email is huge. Getting a person's email shows that they trust you to a certain extent. Don't abuse that trust by sending spam messages or trying to sell to them constantly.

The best way I know to get a person's email is called the "freemium offer." Here's an example of how to execute the freemium offer:

I tell you that I have an email marketing course that's completely free. If you go over to my website right now, you can get that course. It's comprised of six videos that will walk you through the process of setting up an email account with a provider like MailChimp, Aweber, or Infusionsoft. The course will also teach you how to write email subject lines and design the body of your email. But wait, there's more. I'm going to show you how to properly communicate to people, so that you can influence them to buy your product or service. The course is completely free. All you have to do is enter your email on my website and it'll be sent it to your inbox immediately.

Would you give me your email address? Approximately 50-70% of website visitors will say, *"Hell ya!"* as long as the offer seems more valuable than the submission of their email address.

DO NOT try and push your products and services every time you send you an email! This is a big mistake I see a lot of people making. They give away something for free, but their next 60 emails are promotions to buy their product or service. This is that fastest way to lose the trust of your potential customers! They may even report your emails as spam. Then they'll NEVER see your emails and you've lost them for good.

Blogs are great for delivering value to your potential buyers. I have a blog. I often post content to that blog and then send out emails like this:

Subject Line: hey…got something cool to show you
"Hey, I know you're interested in email marketing.
So I just made a video specifically for you and it's a case study. In this case study, I'm going to show you a campaign that I showed a client of mine that generated $10,000 in income for him in about 36 hours!
You can use this same email marketing campaign in your business to get similar results! My gift to you!
Here's the link, check it out!
(link to blog)
Talk soon,
Burf"

Now, here's a question. If you checked out my blog, applied some of the strategy I taught you, and were able to get results from it, would it boost your trust in me? Of course it would!

Frank Kern covers this topic when he discusses Results In Advance (RIA). He advocates giving people value-driven content which helps them get results. If you help them get results, you earn their trust. I mentioned Gary Vaynerchuk before, who refers to this same strategy as "Jab, Jab, Jab, Rght Hook." In case you forgot, "Jab, Jab, Jab" is about giving value-driven content. The right hook is asking for the sell.

If you can earn $1500 from applying information I shared with you in the form of an email, you'll trust me. So what do you think happens if I continually give you results for free, and then one day I come to you with a product or service I'm selling? I'll tell you what happens, because I've seen it work like clockwork over and over again. You're going to buy it. Why?

1: The Law of Reciprocity.
2. Human behavior says that if I give you free stuff that works and gets you a result, logically you'll think to yourself, *"Damn, if the free stuff did that for me, I can only imagine what the paid stuff will do for me."*

As an online marketer, you need to build relationships first. Refrain from poking your potential customers by sending multiple emails asking them to buy from you. They are not going to buy your stuff until they have a relationship with you. We live in an economy where people need to trust you before they buy from you. You need to remember that email addresses are sacred and should be treated with respect.

Here's another important tip: When you send an email, don't generalize. Your emails should be personal. You want the recipient to feel like you are talking to them face-to-face. When I'm speaking to my best friend, it's different than when I'm speaking up on stage to a group of people. People want to feel like you're talking to them directly, even if you're not. They want to feel special. They want feel like you're only talking to them.

I have sent out emails that were so personal that my subscribers couldn't tell if they were mass emails or if they were sent to them personally. Some of my long time subscribers wrote back to me asking, *"Burf, did you send that just to me or did you send that to everyone?"* That's what you want to do with every single email. If you can do that, it strengthens the relationship like nothing else can. Small touches, like simply addressing the person using either their name or using the word "You" make huge differences. For example, you wouldn't want to say:

"Hey everyone, I absolutely love all of my subscribers. You guys are the best. I made this training video for everyone and you can find it over here on my blog."

Instead, the same email should be written like this:

"Hey, I made this really awesome training video for you.
I was thinking about you the other day and I know that you have an interest in email marketing, so I put together this case study that I know you're going to find a lot of value in.
As a matter of fact, all you have to do is click this link and go over to my blog to check it out right now. Let me know what you think about it.
Burf."

Do you see the difference between the two email structures? The second email is a great example of how you should talk to your potential clients or customers - by giving them a sense of belonging. Every time you write an email, imagine there's one person sitting on the other side, not a list of 500, 10,000, or even 100,000. Imagine you're writing to one person directly.

You may feel a small sense of embarrassment from sending more personal emails, but you can be sure that they'll be opened more often than generic mass emails. Intriguing subject lines are also crucial for getting people to open your emails. I have about 60 different subject line formulas that you can access for free on my website -

vanburfmedia.com/subjectlines.

(see what I did there?) LOL. Enjoy!

Chapter 9
Marketing Funnels and the Boiling Frog

"The buyer journey is nothing more than a series of questions that must be answered."
-Analyst Firm IDC

This chapter is all about marketing funnels and the "boiling frog" concept. The boiling frog concept comes from a series of temperature studies conducted on frogs in the late 19th century. When a frog was thrown into a pot of boiling water, it jumped right out thanks to its quick reflexes.

Then, the scientists turned down the heat. They put a frog in cold water and he stayed put. Gradually, they turned up the heat. The frog's cold-bloodedness helped its body adapt to the increasing temperature. Even when the temperature got hot enough to boil the water, the frog didn't notice, since the change was so gradual. The frog sat right in the boiling water, none the wiser.

It all starts with the free offer, the freemium. Maybe you've put together some sort of eBook, a report, a mini course, or a webinar that you're giving away for free. As we discussed previously, you can successfully ask someone to give you their email address in exchange for that freemium.

Once they opt in, accepting the freemium in exchange for their email address, they get redirected to a page where you have what's called a trigger. The trigger offers them something of value at a reduced cost. They would see, for example, a course they could normally buy for $197. Instead, the trigger page has it reduced to $7. It becomes a no-brainer offer for them and they purchase that $7 item.

As soon as they make that purchase, they get redirected to another page that says, *"Hey, before we give you the course that you just bought, we have an-*

other offer for you that you may be interested in. "Now, you offer them something of even more value for lesser cost. Maybe it's a $397 product that you're now offering for just $79. It's another no-brainer. They click the right buttons and their credit card gets charged the $79.

Moving on, you take them to another page where you have something else to offer them. It could be a $1500 product that they can now get for $397. This is the boiling frog concept used in a marketing scenario. Since the prices are gradually rising, they're more easily tolerated.

You bring them in on a low cost offer, then you upsell them to something that's a little bit more expensive. Then, continue heating the water up with something that's a bit more expensive. Of course, your customers aren't hostages. At any point, they have the option of ending their transaction, which sends them over to the $7 product that they purchased initially.

People aren't stupid. They're not going to just keep buying increasingly expensive products if they're not valuable. You need to have rock solid products, a compelling sales message, compelling copy, and maybe a video that really explains the products' benefits for good measure. Marketing funnels and the boiling frog concept can't apply when your products or services don't cut it. You need to put forth something of real value that's going to help somebody at the end of the day.

Most people who end up in abusive relationships will tell you that their relationships didn't start out as being abusive at the beginning. If I took a lady out on a first date and I started slapping her around, she probably wouldn't go on a second date with me.

On the first date, if I portrayed myself as a really nice and sweet guy maybe we would end up more time together. Then if, I started making little verbal jabs at her, she would think I was just playing around. As we continue in the relationship that, mental abuse could gradually get worse to the point where I'm slapping the lady around. At this point, she wouldn't want to leave all of a sudden. She loves me despite my bad behavior! I've gradually taken her through the process of loving me. This is how a lot of abusive relationships start out and ultimately end up. While it's a terrible thing that happens too often, this scenario illustrates the same concept extremely well.

When a CEO hires a new employee who they want to eventually take over their business, they're not going to have them take the reigns right away. Such an employee goes through a process of being trained in various areas of the business until it's time for them to completely take over - only after being prepared for it.

An athlete training for a marathon doesn't set out for the marathon the moment he makes up his mind. He has to work on his stamina, build his muscles, and get stronger over an extended period of time until he's ready to go run that marathon. The stress would be too much without the gradual build-up.

That's how these marketing funnel works on the human psyche. Their effectiveness comes from gradual build up with help from triggers and low-cost offers. It works best when you have something really low-cost - cheap enough to make them pull out their credit card, enter their information, and purchase that first product. Then, we heat the water up slowly.

The Facebook ad campaign is a good place to get people to enter your marketing funnel. At VanBurf Media, we give out free eBooks on our page by providing a link to download them. Of course, this can only happen once you enter you name and email on our website to gain instant access. Once an interested customer does this, they are automatically thrown into the funnel.

If you've never used a funnel, ClickFunnels.com gives you access to some templates that will make it easy for you to build your first one.

Chapter 10
The Lamborghini Close

"Price is what you pay, value is what you get"
-Warren Buffet

Value comes first. Your customers or clients must see value in what you are offering. Always ask yourself, *"Is my product providing enough value to justify its price?"* If people perceive that the value your product offers is greater than its price, they won't hesitate to click that "Buy" button.

It's story-time again. This time, I'll tell you my Lamborghini Close story.

A few years back, I was involved in a network marketing company. It all started with Bill Lewis, a chiropractor and friend of mine from my email list. Bill emailed me and told me he had been an ardent follower of mine for years. He also told me that he was coming to Dallas, Texas for a seminar. He wanted to meet me in person, so he invited me to dinner and said he wanted to "pick my brain."

I'm always enthusiastic about meeting new people, especially those who have been loyal followers. Bill had purchased many of my online products and courses in the past, so I told him I would gladly meet up with him. At dinner, we spoke extensively about business, entrepreneurship, and online marketing. Over dinner, Bill presented me with an opportunity to get involved in a network marketing company that he was in. Although I wasn't sure about it at first, I ended up telling him I would give it a shot.

When I make a decision to get involved in something, I go all-in. I don't do anything half-assed. In my first eight months at the network marketing company, I recruited over a thousand people into my organization. I was doing home events and giving presentations 4-5 times a day, 7 days a week. I put 38,000 miles on my car in 8 months driving around to various meetings. Needless to say, I got really good at presenting my message and and closing people.

During this period, I developed what I call the "Lamborghini Close." Towards the end of my 30-minute presentation, I'd say to a room full of people, *"If I drove up in a brand new Lamborghini and told you that you could have this $250,000 vehicle for $400, how many of you here right now would take me up on that deal?"* Every single hand in the room went up.

Now, keep in mind that the product I was selling had a price tag of exactly $400. The name of the product was Builder Pack. I used that $400 number specifically because that was the investment they were going to have to make to get into this network marketing company.

After asking if the people in the room would purchase my Lamborghini for $400, I would pick one person in the crowd to speak to directly - usually someone I had met while mingling before the meeting. One time, I chose a guy named Mike.

I said, *"Mike, you obviously want this Lamborghini for 400 bucks right? What if I told you that you had 48 hours to get the $400? Could you do it?"* His response? *"Hell ya I could do it!!"* He was willing to go the extra mile to get that $400. Whether it be from his savings, borrowing from his parents, having a yard sale, or selling his plasma, he was willing to do whatever it took. Mike saw that the Lamborghini's value was far greater than its price, so small obstacles to obtaining $400 wouldn't stop him.

After walking the room through the Lamborghini scenario, I would explain to my audience that what I was really offering them wasn't a Builder Pack. What I was really offering them was an opportunity to get into a business that could potentially afford them the luxury to be able buy cars like Lamborghinis. I knew guys that had bought Bentleys and Lamborghinis with money they earned from the network company they worked for. I painted a picture for my audience to show them that network marketing was a vehicle that could get them to where they wanted to go in life. I persisted in telling them that with a $400 investment, they would have the opportunity of making a 6-figure income - if they were willing to put in the work to get there.

Of course, I would also tell them that those types of results were not typical. The results they would see from their work depended on how much work, time, and effort (not to mention blood, sweat, and tears) they were willing to put into it.

At that time, I was putting in 90 hours a week non-stop to build my business. I often get asked by people how I became so successful. I had a guy ask me one time, *"Dude, it seem like everything you touch turns to gold. How do you do it?"* I asked, "Do *you* want the truth?" He said, *"Of course."* I told him, *"I fail more than everyone else. But I work harder than everyone else. And I never quit."*

The Lamborghini Close was so effective because it gave people a new way to view my product. It wasn't just $400 anymore. The product's $400 price tag was cheap compared to the potential that the product represented.

Eben Pagan, a mentor of mine and an extremely successful online marketer, once said that when he was a kid, he always thought that if he could get a million people to give him a dollar, then he would be a millionaire. As a young teenager, he would sit around daydreaming, thinking of ways to scheme people into giving him a dollar. Over time, though, he realized his mindset was flawed. It was a scarcity mindset. Asking people to give you a dollar and not offering any form of value in return is a broke mindset. From that, he learned that if he could give $100 worth of value and ask people for $10 in return, they would be willing to give him $10 every time. His mindset expanded to, *"If I could give a million people $100 worth of value and ask them for $10 in return, then I would become a deca-millionaire."* And he achieved just that.

That's the kind of mindset you need to have when you're selling your product or service. Give them more value than they're actually paying for. When you master that fundamental strategy, your business will explode.

Chapter 11
Getting an Advantage with an Avatar

"Our jobs as marketers are to understand how the customer wants to buy and help them do so."
-Bryan Eisenberg

Many years ago, I had the privilege of getting to know Frank Kern. He's helped me earn millions of dollars selling products online. Obviously, my respect for the man is immense. One of the things he taught me was how to get an advantage by considering my Avatar - my ideal prospect. In this chapter, I'll pass on Frank's knowledge. I'll be showing you an exercise on how to create your own personal Avatar. Kern uses the term "Core Customer" for the same purpose as "Avatar."

I'll ask a series of questions that will help you create your avatar, but don't answer them now. After reading this chapter, come back and write down the answers to each of the questions asked here.

Some of these questions are going to sound weird. Chances are, you're going to ask, *"What the hell does the color of eyes or the color off the hair have to do with making money?"* Just have a little faith and trust me. It will all come together by the end.

So, here are the questions:

Is your Avatar male or female?

What is the name of your Avatar? (First weird question, I know. But it helps. The more detail you picture your Avatar with, the better. So what's their name? Is it Mike? Carol? Nicole? Sean?)

How old are they? (Be specific. Don't say "45-55 years old." Pick one single age. For example, 38 years old.)

What hair color do they have?

What is their eye color?

What is their skin tone?

How many children do they have?

Do they work?

If they work, are they self-employed?

If they're not self-employed, who do they work for? What is their position in the company?

What is their household income?

What kind of clothes do they like to wear? (For example, *"They like to wear athletic wear, like t-shirts and sweatpants."*)

What kind of house do they live in? (One story? Two Story? Cape Cod style or ranch style?)

What is their favorite food?

Are they married? If so, what is their spouse like?

What are their friends like?

What time do they go to bed every night?

(Remember, as we create our Avatars - our ideal prospects - we're designing one perfect person that we can keep in mind as we conduct our marketing and craft our messages.)

What kind of spousal problems are they experiencing, if any?

What type of financial problems are they dealing with on a daily, weekly, and monthly basis?

What kinds of health problems do they have, if any?

If they have children, how do they act around their children normally? What about when they're suffering from their problems (health-related, spousal, financial, etc.)?

If they have a spouse, how do they act around their spouse normally? What about when they're suffering from their problems (health-related, spousal, financial, etc.)?

(As a business owner and entrepreneur, you get paid to solve problems. If somebody has a problem and you have a product or service that can solve that problem, people will pay you handsomely for your life-changing product or service. Of course, that's if they believe you can actually solve their problem. You have to be able to communicate and demonstrate that you can. It all starts with understanding your customers on a deep level. You need to find out what types of problems they may be experiencing in their lives. Health, relationship, and financial problems are just examples, but we all know that the number of potential problems in life is endless.)

Back to our questions...

How does their problem affect them only on a daily basis?

Does the problem impact their sex life? If so, how?

(Financial stress and health problems often cause people to lose intimacy with each other. Financial debt and the stress that comes as a result represent one of the largest causes for divorce.)

Have they consulted any professionals for help with this problem?

What kind of emotions do they experience because of this problem?

What options have they considered to solve this problem?

What is their surface-level desire regarding this problem?

What is their deep-seeded desire regarding this problem?

What are their three biggest frustrations regarding this problem?

What are the three biggest emotions their problem is causing?

(i.e. financial problems may result in fear of losing their home)

These questions help us get ultra specific about the type of prospect we want to attract with our business. Now, in order for this to work, we must genuinely be able to empathize with this person; we need to identify with them and and know exactly what they're going through. It's crucial to to know what their surface desire outcome is and their real (deep seeded) desired outcome is. The deep-seeded desire is what they really want.

For example, when people are in pain and they go to a doctor, it's usually not just the pain that they want to get rid of. Of course, they don't want to be in pain. The relief of their pain, however, is just the surface desired outcome. The deep-seeded desire is about what the pain is taking away from them. It's about what they want to get back when their pain is relieved.

Having a migraine for 15 hours might cause your Avatar to miss her child's graduation. Maybe those migraines headaches ruined your Avatar's trip to Disney World because she layed in her hotel room for 3 of her trip's 5 days.

When you craft your message to your avatar, you have to know exactly who they are. You must genuinely care about them and want to help them. If you don't care about the person on the other side, none of this is going to work. If you are only about getting the money, this book isn't for you.

I'm not here just to help you grow your business. I wrote this book to help you genuinely help more people with your products and services. Your venture is not all about you. If you want to be really successful in business and in life, you have to have a purpose that's bigger than yourself.

Person-to-person communication is the most effective way to sell and increase your closing ratios online. This is why I took you through this exercise. This exercise was designed to help you create that one, single person you're going to communicate with directly by using your marketing.

You are not going to market to everyone. When you speak to everyone, you speak to no one. Each message you craft will be designed to speak to one person - your Avatar.

The next step is to take the data you've collected by answering the questions I asked and use them to construct a story about your avatar. I want you to get crystal-clear on who this person is. You should be able to close your eyes and envision EXACTLY who this person is. See the color of their eyes, the color of their hair, how many kids they have, where they work, what clothes they wear, the problems they experience, the emotional roller coaster they're on, and their deepest desires.

To help you, I'll share a story I constructed for my Avatar, Kylie. I am not a chiropractor, but I used to own a chiropractic office years ago. I had several Avatars for my office, one for each health condition we wanted to market to. Without any further ado, I'd like you to meet Kylie, my Migraine Headache Avatar.

Kylie is a 38 year old stay-at-home mom. She has big brown eyes and long brown hair. She likes to wear comfy clothes around the house, like t-shirts and leggings. When she goes on date nights with her husband or nights out with her friends, though, she likes to dress up. Kylie has two children: Grace is 8 and Jacob is 6. She's happily married to her husband

Caleb (42). Caleb is the CEO of his own Pest Control company. Kylie and Caleb have disposable income. Kylie makes her own healthcare decisions.

Kylie is open to natural forms of health care like chiropractic and acupuncture. She only takes drugs and medication as a last resort. Over the last 5 years, though, taking meds has become normal for Kylie.

Kylie experiences migraine headaches every week, sometimes lasting as long as 2 or 3 days. When her migraines hit, Kylie has to retreat to a dark room and tell the kids to not make any loud noises. She often gets nauseous with her migraines and sometimes she even has to throw up violently.

Kylie takes a drug for her migraines, but it gives her side effects like dizziness and acid reflux. She feels like she has no control over her migraines and certain aspects of her life. More than anything else, Kylie wants to regain control of the situation - and her life.

When her migraines hit, Kylie can't think straight; all she can think about is getting rid of the migraine. When Kylie has a migraine, she can't help but ignore her children completely. Later, this makes her feel terribly guilty. She feels like she's a bad mother. Kylie's biggest fear is that one day her children will look back and say, *"Mom wasn't there for us."* Kylie is afraid to admit she's not the mom she should be.

Kylie hasn't been intimate with her husband Caleb for over a year, largely due to the frequency of her migraines. The lack of intimacy has caused a lot of stress and strained their marriage. Kylie tries to pretend that her migraines don't affect her ability to be the best mom and best wife ever, but it's clear that they do.

Kylie wants to be able to live her life without taking medication for her migraines. She wants to live without the fear of a migraine hitting her at any moment. It's important for Kylie to know that she can be there for her children and her husband when they need her. She doesn't want to feel guilty about retreating to a dark room when her migraines hit. She wants to feel normal again.

Now you know Kylie. Any time I crafted a message for people with migraines, I imagined I was speaking directly to Kylie. I wasn't thinking about the millions of people that suffer from migraines. I was only thinking about Kylie.

Here's some copy I wrote for a migraine ad we ran in the newspaper of our community (back when newspaper ads were still effective LOL).

"You're a stay-at-home mom with two screaming kids while you suffer from devastatingly painful migraine headaches two to three times per week that make you nauseated and make you want to hide in a dark soundproof room for the next 24 hours.

What can you do when you've tried everything?

First of all, I want you to know that you're not alone, We've helped hundreds of stay-at-home moms suffering from migraine headaches just like you and we achieved this without drugs, injections or surgery.

I understand how you feel with these migraines, and what you're going through. Our number one goal is to help you live a normal life again.

I also realize that when your migraines hit with a vengeance and you have to crawl into a dark soundproof room just to cope with the pain, that it sometimes causes you to feel guilty about not being there for your kids.

I know you want to be the best mom you can be. So don't feel guilty. It's not your fault. It's your call, but I think we should at least talk. Call us today to schedule your free consultation."

You might have noticed that that ad was completely designed around my avatar. I was able to put myself in her shoes, understand what she was going through, and craft my message to appeal to her, specifically.

Maybe you're thinking right now, *"I don't really know that much about what my avatar might be going through. It's going to be hard for me to complete this exercise."* Here's a tip: use Google and Facebook.

You can search through forums, groups, blogs, and Facebook pages surrounding your niche. Using these public spaces, you can gather bits of information about some of the challenges people are facing in your marketplace and the emotional challenges they are going through as a result. No matter what industry you're in, all you need to do is carry out some research on the problem you're trying to solve.

If you implement this strategy into your business, I promise you'll gain a major advantage over everyone else in your industry. You'll also see a major difference in the type of people you attract with your business. You'll gain more qualified leads. You'll attract people who are at their wits end looking for a solution to their problem, now!

Those people - the ones you can help with their problem now - are the people that are ready to pull the trigger and hire you. Be ready to REALLY help them, because at the end of the day, you still need to get them results. You still need to be able to deliver the goods.

Chapter 12
The Mere Exposure Effect

"The power of visibility can never be underestimated."
-Margret Cho

Mirror, mirror, on the wall, who's the best marketer of them all? When I first heard about the "mere exposure" effect, I thought it was "mirror exposure" effect. The mere exposure effect is a psychological strategy you can employ in your marketplace to position you as an expert and a go-to authority.

This effect is a psychological phenomenon by which people tend to develop a preference for things merely because they are familiar with them. In social psychology, the mere exposure effect is sometimes called the familiarity principle. Basically, when people see something continuously, they tend to feel comfortable with it and even develop a preference for it.

Taking advantage of the mere exposure effect can have a tremendous impact on your business. The best part of it is that you can use a strategy to exploit mere exposure and get great results very, very quickly.

Facebook is where all the attention is, right? People are logged into Facebook day and night. When I drive down the road, I literally see other people driving while surfing Facebook. It's scary as fuck, but it's also reality.

When you go out in public and look around, you see that most people have their faces buried in their smartphones. Chiropractors call this famous posture "text neck." Our collective smartphone addiction has made us all skilled multi-taskers; we can do almost any activity while checking our Facebooks at the same time. As we mentioned in a previous chapter, it's extremely common for people to watch their favorite TV shows and browse Facebook simultaneously. Facebook today's attention marketplace.

Of course, if you want to get attention, you have to go where the attention is. One of the best ways you can do that is by running Facebook video ads in the newsfeed. Produce multiple pieces of content and run ads for them in the newsfeed concurrently. People will constantly be seeing you. Remember: marketing is about reminding people that you exist. It's not their job to remember you; it's your job to remind them.

The more videos and the more ads you can run concurrently, the better. Make videos with free tips, strategies, and ideas that can benefit your audience and help them get results as soon as possible. Doing this will earn your brand massive exposure. By putting out videos week after week, more and more people will consume your content.

If you're a local business owner, how many business owners in your community or industry are running Facebook Video Ads? It's been my experience that very few brick-and-mortar style businesses are leveraging Facebook Video Ads to promote their businesses.

So, what kind of content do you put in these videos? I mentioned tips, strategies, and ideas, but let's get specific. There are several strategies you can use, but a simple and effective strategy to start off with is the Q&A (Question & Answer) video. Write down the most commonly asked questions people ask in your niche or even about your product - then answer them.

For example, if you're a divorce attorney that caters to men, answer questions that men have about divorce. Some examples might be, *"Do I have to give up 50% of everything I own?" "What are my chances of getting full custody my kids?"* and *"Do I have to pay child support if I have shared custody of my kids?"* Asking these questions and then answering them on video could provide heaps of value to men looking for divorce lawyers.

Now, here's a question for you: When was the last time you saw a series of sponsored Facebook Video Ads appearing in your newsfeed from another divorce attorney? Probably never. It's simply not common.

OK let's get even more specific and talk numbers. Make four videos this month of 60-90 seconds in length. That's one video per week. Run a Facebook Video Ad campaign with them. Spend around $300 this month and you can reach 30,000 people in your community for 30 days..

Next month, make four additional videos answering a new series of questions. Now, you have eight videos that people will have seen in their newsfeed. What do you think happens in month three? That's right, make four more videos. Now, twelve videos have run in the newsfeed. Create four new videos every month, all year round. By the end of the year, you will have had 52 different videos appear in the Facebook newsfeed of your community with your brand and your message.

Do this and you will absolutely benefit from the mere exposure effect!

People in your community will have seen you over and over again in their newsfeed for an entire year! Thanks to the mere exposure effect, when people see you over and over again, they tend to have a preference for you. They will feel like they have a relationship with you and your brand. They will feel like they can trust you above everyone else because they will have been exposed to you all year round.

If you want to become an expert in your niche or become the go-to authority that everybody looks up to and trusts, you have to start putting content out there and making sure people are seeing you every single day. Remember, marketing is not about people remembering that you exist; marketing is about reminding people you exist.

This is a strategy you can implement immediately. Taking advantage of the mere exposure effect is cheap and easy thanks to today's social media. Best of all, it will provide your business with tremendous growth. Go! Make those videos now!

Chapter 13
Ten Killer Online Marketing Strategies

"Marketing is no longer about the stuff that you make, but the stories you tell."
-Seth Godin

Your business' success depends on generating more leads and selling more products and services. The best way to do that is to spread your unique message to the world, get your ideas to stick, and manufacture desire and trust in your niche. If you can communicate your message effectively, you can create an insanely loyal tribe of followers who will be happy to spend money on anything you offer.

It's all about building your brand, and that's what this book is all about. Already in this book, we've discussed a number of strategies in great depth. In this chapter, we're going to step back and get a bit lighter.

If you've been around online marketing at all, you're familiar with top 10 lists. Lists like these are great ways to express ideas quickly and simply - and they always seem to get plenty of attention.

This list is my Top 10 Killer Online Marketing Strategies. They'll help you build your brand and stay out of obscurity.

----

1. Partnering with Allies

John D. Rockefeller once said, *"Competition is a sin."* When I first got into online marketing, I saw other marketers as competitors. I didn't want to be associated with them and I certainly didn't want to partner with them. I wanted to be a lone ranger. I wanted to position myself as the expert and show everybody else how much better I was than them.

Over time, though, I began to see the value in partnering with others in my niche. I was able to create mutually beneficial relationships with people I would have previously seen as my competitors. By working with others, I grew my brand and helped them grow their brands at the same time. It was a "Win-Win" for everyone.

As soon as I saw the light and realized that every chance to partner with others in my niche represented a tremendous opportunity for growth, I started working with other marketers.

I've been marketing online to chiropractors since 2006. Over the last few years, however, my brand has branched out beyond just chiropractic. My Facebook Ad Agency, VanBurf Media, now helps all sorts of small business owners and entrepreneurs grow their brands to generate more sales online. We run Facebook Ads for realtors, dentists, financial advisors, orthodontists, plastic surgeons, and everyone in-between.

In the beginning, though, when I was solely in the chiropractic niche, I would go to other marketers and say, *"Hey, I've been reading your blog content and watching your videos. I think you have a lot of value to offer. Would you mind if I sent an email to my list about this blog post of yours that I just read?"* Every marketer wants a larger audience; I was offering value for nothing in return.

As the other marketers continued producing content, I kept on asking them for permission to send out emails about their content. Of course, I was always granted permission.

Later, I found out one marketer I had been approaching had an affiliate program for a product that he was selling. The marketer's name was Matt and his product was focused on how to use social media to grow your chiropractic office. I reached out to Matt and told him I would like to be an affiliate for that program. He agreed. The commission on each sale was 40%.

Eventually, I created my own online marketing course. I approached Matt and I said, *"Hey, I've got this online course and here's what it does. Would you like to be an affiliate of that and send a few emails to your list?"* Matt responded positively to my proposal and sent out emails to his entire database about my product and what I had to offer. He drove people over to an opt-in where they could give their email to access a free training I had.

As a result of Matt's help, tons of people opted in to my list. My email list started to grow exponentially. That was the first affiliate deal that I had done where I had partnered with an ally. I did around $36,000 in sales from the launch of that online course. From that day forward, I looked at Matt and other marketers in the profession as allies instead of as competition.

Partnering with Matt really helped me get my name out there. Matt was a marketer of high caliber. The people on his list knew him, liked him, and trusted him. They knew that if Matt was going out of his way to mention me, I had to have some value from which they could benefit. Their expectations were high. Luckily, I didn't disappoint.

If you're a small business owner with a brick and mortar business, you need to think about who you can partner with in your community. Don't be too picky; you could partner with your local dry cleaner, a yoga studio, or a gym. If you help enough people out, people will eventually return the favor and help you out.

2. Embrace User-Generated Content

I've discovered many times that as online marketers, our egos are often formidable foes. When we're seen as experts and authorities, our heads get big! We get carried away by our success and can be prone to forgetting our followers - the ones that made our success possible in the first place.

You need to pay attention to your customers, clients, and followers online. If you really want to go deep with your audience, engage with the content they post. Like their posts, comment on them, and even share them. This will show that you are a real human being that cares about what they have to say.

Have you ever made a post on Facebook that no one "liked?" It feels shitty.

On the flip side, imagine how good it would have felt if someone you truly admired "liked" your post. For example, I'm a huge fan of Frank Kern. If I made a post on Facebook and Frank Kern took the time to comment on my post or just simply "like" it, I would be ecstatic! I would screen capture it, draw a big red circle and a huge red arrow pointing to his name, and I would repost it with a status update that says, *"None, of ya'll liked my post, but FRANK KERN liked my post, beyotches!!"*

It feels good when other people engage with your content. Make sure you're taking the time to give back to your audience by engaging with their content, too.

3. Collaborate with Influencers

You probably understand that "influencers" are people and brands that other people listen to in their community or niche. If an influencer recommends a product, people will buy that product.

Every community has influencers. If you don't know who the influencers are in your community, you need to find out. Let's say you're a small business owner in Allen, Texas. Influencers in your community might include the mayor, somebody on the city council, a local gym owner, and maybe professional (or semi-professional) athletes or sports teams.

Influencers are well known and have the respect of the people that look up to them; the potential value of collaborating with them should be obvious. Collaborating with influencers is a lot like gaining followers, though. You must be willing to give to them first. Give without expecting them to give back. Remember the Law of Reciprocity? It comes into play with influencers, too.

A great way to give value to influencers is to ask them directly, *"How can I help you?"* Let them know you have a Facebook Following and an email list. If they would like, you can let your followers know about them. Once the influencer gives you the go-ahead, make a post promoting the influencer. This type of tactic was mentioned in the first strategy, "Partnering with Allies." Influencers are the best kinds of allies.

If the influencer you wish to collaborate with is local, you could go old school. Stop by their place of business or their facility and offer a token of your appreciation. You could give them an Amazon gift card, movie tickets, or a basket of cookies. Let your imagination run wild! In many cases, the weirder your gift is, the better.

4. Help Your Followers Solve Their Problems

Frank Kern calls this a "Goodwill Campaign." Like many other of my favorite strategies, this one comes down to delivering value-driven content.

The best content - from blog posts to videos - does a couple main things. It captures peoples' attention. It also helps people solve their problems by anticipating common pain-points and offering solutions - free of charge.

Dr. Josh Axe is a nutritionist and chiropractor with a YouTube channel. Josh has made a wide variety of videos like "5 Steps To Heal A Leaky Gut," "Natural Treatment For Sleep Apnea," and many more. He started producing this content back in 2012. People appreciated Josh's videos so much that they commented, liked, and shared them. His popularity grew organically and he now has over a million subscribers.

I once watched Josh do a Facebook Live video. He had over 50,000 people tune in. Josh's popularity is a result of his ability to solve people's problems. People are especially attracted to Josh because he refrains from gimmicky partial solutions. So many people offer partial solutions and then expect payment for the second half. Josh knows better than to turn his followers off like that.

Josh owns a brand called Ancient Nutrition. The brand's main product is Bone Broth Protein. People purchase Josh's products because they've built trust with him and they know that his recommendations bring about tangible solutions. Last year, his company made over $100,000,000! Yes, that's 100 Million Dollars - and he just started his company in 2012.

5. Let Your Customers Interact with You

A lot of business owners make the decision to keep their Facebook profile pages private. For example, a lot of chiropractors don't want their patients being their friends on Facebook. They believe their professional lives should be separated from their private lives. I can certainly understand this believe, but it's a huge mistake in my opinion.

Instead, let your customers become friends with you and interact with you on various social media platforms. If you do this, you can begin to go deep with them.

6. Experiment with New Channels and Platforms

Earlier in this book, I discussed explained that you don't need to create entirely new content for every platform. Instead, you can repurpose your content from Facebook and distribute it on other platforms channels like YouTube, Twitter, Instagram, Snapchat, Instagram Stories, Facebook Stories, and Facebook Messenger, among others.

For example, I publish content on iTunes (my podcast is Propaganda Marketing Machine) because I'm aware that some people prefer to listen to my content rather than read it or watch it in video format. Many people love to listen to audio content on their commutes; they want to consume content even on the move, and I've made it easy for them to get access to it.

I also post video content on YouTube and to my Instagram account. You'll find out that I post similar content because I want to make sure I'm consistent with what I'm putting out there.

7. Have Fun!

Don't be afraid to get a little goofy and let your personality shine when creating your content! A brand's personality is far more important than many people understand. It's more important than a logo or a slogan, by far.

You should aim at getting people to fall in love with your brand by making it easy for them to fall in love with the personality of the brand. The only way you can really do that is to just have some good, old fashioned fun. Don't be stiff. And don't take yourself so damn serious all the time.

8. Get Your Employees Involved

Sue B. Zimmerman once owned a boutique in Cape Cod named SueBDoo, but now she teaches Instagram. During her boutique ownership days, she found that her employees were often taking selfies at work. In fact, they spent a large percentage of their time on social media. Sue decided to leveage her employees' addiction to social media for her business. She made a new rule: *"No cellphones while you're working - except when you're doing something that promotes our business."*

Sue told her staff that during their downtime at work, they could get dressed up in some of the boutique's clothing, take pictures of themselves, and post them on Facebook and Instagram. When Sue implemented her new rule, she saw a significant increase in her sales - about 15 to 20 percent. Her quirky rule became a form of advertisement for her brand.

If you have employees, they're an essential part of your business. They have personality to offer. You need to find out what you can do to get them involved in building your brand.

9. Get a Little Weird

Believe it or not, weird is attractive. We have been made to believe that being weird is bad. Actually, being weird is what sets you apart from everybody else.

I once ran a Facebook Ad for a chiropractor in Sherman, Texas named Keith Kimberlin. It was video ad that showed him demonstrating an adjustment. He practices a little known technique called AMIT (Advanced Muscle Integration Technique). It's a weird technique, but it gets results like nothing I've ever seen.

The headline I used for the ad was, "Weird Chiropractic Technique Fixes Man's Chronic Knee Pain." The ad was a huge success! It generated 18 new patients in one month. Even better, 17 of those patients got even further invested with a chiropractic care program. The new business generated by the video translated to about $68,000 in revenue - not too shabby for a weird ad.

10. Don't Forget Your Current Customers

Sometimes, we get so involved in trying to get new customers and build our clientele that we forget about the current ones. Occasionally, you should do something really special for your current customer base. One example would be a "Customer Appreciation Day."

If you own a brick and mortar type of business, a Customer Appreciation Day may involve decorating the business, serving food and drinks, and maybe offering something of value like a gift card that gives them 25% off any product or service you offer.

If you're an online marketer, you could do a good, old fashioned 50% OFF your online course in a "Follower Appreciation Sale." The point is:

never forget to take care of the people that take care of you.

I was at Dillard's recently and saw a nice pair of Versace sunglasses. I tried them on, took a picture, and posted it to Facebook, saying, *"Hey, so what do you guys think? Should I get them?"* One of my clients said I looked fantastic in them but I shouldn't get them yet. I agreed.

Two weeks later, I received those sunglasses in the mail with a note that said, *"Thank you for doing everything that you do for us and for helping us grow our business. I don't know what I'd do without you. Enjoy your sunglasses."* I was blown away by this act of generosity. I realized I needed to show more generosity, myself - to my own clients.

One of my clients likes to go deep sea fishing. Last year, I bought him a pair of $500 cufflinks that had a shark's head on it. He posted it the cufflinks to Facebook, just like I did with the sunglasses I received. I gave another client an autographed Joe Namath, NY Jets Jersey. Of course, you don't need to get something expensive for your customers like I did. You do, however, need to take care of your them from time to time.

Frank Kern sent me a huge coffee mug with his logo on it. That mug probably cost him $3 but I felt so special when I opened the mail that day. I thought, *"Frank Kern fucking rocks!"*

Don't misunderstand. This chapter is not a substitute for the entire book. People love top ten lists, though, so there you go. Those are my top ten strategies for building your brand through online marketing.

Chapter 14
Don't Get Caught in the Monkey Fist Trap

"Some of us think holding on makes us strong; but sometimes it is letting go."
-Hermann Hesse

The "Monkey Fist Trap" is a technique used for monkey-hunting in Africa. Natives set their trap by making a hole in a tree or stump. Then, they put a nut inside the hole. When a monkey notices the nut, it sticks its hand in the hole to grab the nut. With the nut in its hand, the monkey's hand forms a fist that is larger than the opening of the hole. The monkey can't pull its fist out while holding the nut. It'll sit there, jerking and pulling, trying to get the nut out of the tree tirelessly. The natives will then literally walk right up to the monkey and bop it on the head with a stick. The monkey won't let go of the nut even at the expense of its own life.

The monkey's inability to let go of the nut is an excellent demonstration of the scarcity mindset. The monkey is blinded by his greed. The nut in its hand makes it forget the possibility of all other nuts. Of course, the monkey could easily let the nut go. run away, and get another nut somewhere. Instead, the monkey loses its life as a result of the scarcity mindset.

One question I get from online marketers all the time is, *"Chris, how much value should I give away for free? I don't want to get into a position where I just give away my best stuff and then nobody wants to buy what I have to offer because I've already given it to them."* The thinking that leads to this question is what I call "getting caught in the monkey trap." You're so scarcity-minded that you're thinking giving value is dangerous to your bottom line. You think that by giving away extreme value to people, they won't want to buy your product or request your services. You're afraid of giving up value so you end up putting out mediocre content that has very little or no value.

The fact is: if I give away my most valued content, people are actually going to buy more stuff from me. This is the lesson I learned a long time ago from Eben Pagan and Frank Kern, two of the top online marketers in the world today. Pagan and Kern taught me early on that when you put out content, you should give away your best information.

Most people think that if they give away their best stuff, there won't be anything left for them to sell. Actually, when you give away your best information, it generally leads to a significant increase in sales. Giving away your best content manufactures desire and trust in your marketplace. You position yourself as an expert and authority in your niche. Ultimately, you sell a lot more of your shit.

Dr. Chris Zaino is a good friend of mine. Chris has one of the largest practices in the history of chiropractic. He offers an online program which he calls "The Dynamic Dinner." The program teaches chiropractors how to do dinner workshops in their communities. When chiropractors conduct dinner workshops, they invite their patients to a free dinner event at a local restaurant. Patients are encouraged to bring guests to the dinner. A presentation on health is given. At the end of the presentation, the hosts give the guests an opportunity to schedule an appointment and meet with the chiropractor for consultation and examination.

Dr. Zaino sells this program that shows chiropractors how to market and perform one of these presentations. When he first launched this product, he gave away three extremely valuable videos. Those three videos literally taught people the entire system. You might wonder, *"What's left to teach? He gave away everything!"* Dr. Z went on to do multiple six figures in sales!

Don't be afraid to give away the value. Don't be afraid to let go of the nut; letting go of the nut helps you build trust with your audience and earn the right to position yourself as an expert and authority in your community.

Chapter 15
Manufacturing Desire and Trust

"Most good relationships are built on mutual trust and respect."
-Mona Sutphen

Every business owner wants his customers to anticipate his products. But where does it come from? That anticipation, that desire, that trust that your product will be worth the wait - it's up to you as a business owner to manufacture it.

In this chapter, I'm going to walk you through a strategy that's going to show you how to manufacture desire for your products and services - the kind of desire that keeps your customers on their toes, always waiting for your new content and products.

I learned this strategy from the legend himself: Frank Kern. Frank showed me the way many years ago and it's helped me generate millions of dollars in online sales. Read carefully and implement properly, and you'll be able to replicate my results.

Remember RIA - Results In Advance? The purpose of RIA is to deliver results to potential customers - right away. You have to give people advice, tips, strategies, or ideas that will solve their problems or benefit them in some way, and you have to do this before asking for anything in return. If you can provide RIA, your followers will look at you like a god! RIA manufactures a deep, burning desire to purchase whatever product or service you're offering.

Here's an analogy that will explain this strategy quite nicely:

Before a romantic relationship can be established, a young man and a young lady have to meet each other. Then, they must exchange phone numbers so that they can communicate with each other and possibly schedule their first date. Once they go on the date (or perhaps multiple dates), the young man has to score his first kiss. After the first lip-lock, maybe the couple gets to know each other better and progresses into a steady relationship. Ultimately, the end goal of their relationship might be marriage. If we look at the wedding as the final achievement, it's clear to see that a young man has to get through many challenges leading up to marriage.

First, in order to talk to a girl, he has to learn how to approach girls. So, if I'm selling an online course that teaches guys how to meet girls, I might offer some sort of tip or advice on how to approach a girl in any situation. Whether it's at the grocery store, at the club, at the gym or wherever, my tip will help young men everywhere make a successful approach. One young man might see my free advice and say, *"Okay, here's what I got to do. I'm going to muster up the courage to talk to the girl at the gym."*

So, he takes the advice that I give him. He approaches the girl and it goes well. The girl says to herself, *"Wow, this guy seems really nice."* But the guy hasn't thought this far ahead yet. He's thinking, *"Holy crap. Now what do I do? I don't know. There wasn't a next step. What do I do?"*

Naturally, the young man consults me for advice. He goes back to my content and finds a video that provides tips on how to get a lady's phone number. He watches it and heads back to the gym full of confidence. This time, he approaches the girl and says, *"Hey, would you mind if I gave you a call sometime or maybe texted you? I really enjoyed our conversation the other day and would like to hang out with you more."* And she says yes!

Now I've helped this dude talk to the girl he's been admiring from afar and I helped him get her phone number. My content helped him achieve his goals. He will see me as a relationship and communication expert. I've provided RIA.

As we discussed before, though, getting a girl's phone number isn't the end of the journey. I've helped this young man get the girl's phone number, but he's going to need more information on how to take this relationship to the next level. So, let's say I offer him a course on how to cultivate a meaningful relationship with the girl of his dreams. He's going to buy that course because he's made it this far based off the free advice that I've given him. It all comes from delivering RIA - results in advance.

This is why it's critical that you give people your best tips and advice and not hold anything back.

Giving people immense value for free makes them like you. They trust you and develop a desire to consume anything you create. For example, if I was a chiropractor targeting people with migraine headaches, I might offer a free report. "Here are the top five causes of migraines and the top five myths that most people buy into when treating them." When my customers read that report, they say, "*Wow, that sounds like a lot of the things that I've been doing wrong, I wonder what else this doctor has to say?*"

Then, I would create a video mini-series providing people with tips and advice on how to prevent migraines naturally. I might show them some sleeping positions that help support the curvature in their neck at night (research shows most migraines and headaches stem from problems in the cervical spine). Maybe, I would show them a series of pressure points they can apply. After giving them this content, they try some of the techniques and now they're starting to build trust with me because they tried some of them and they worked! Eventually, they call and schedule an appointment with me. I helped them get relief, but what about a permanent solution? Since I was able to help so much for free, I must be able to work wonders with a real consultation.

Spend some time today and think about what type of results in advance you can deliver to your marketplace to build that desire and trust that you're looking for. Desire and trust that allows you to charge as much as you want for the solution that you have to offer.

Chapter 16
Practical Value vs Intrinsic Value

"Creativity is the process of having original ideas that have value. It is a process; it's not random."
-Ken Robinson

The need for a value-driven product cannot be overemphasized. Value is the main factor that will determine your product's success. In Chapter 14, we talked about not getting stuck in the monkey trap. Avoid the scarcity mindset and don't fear giving up value. Instead, offer as much as you can to build likeability, trust, desire and position yourself as an expert and authority in your marketplace.

In this chapter, we'll dive deeper and look at the difference between practical value and intrinsic value. Practical value is the actual utility of something while intrinsic value is more complicated. Intrinsic value is where you really begin to build the desire. If you can offer high intrinsic value, you can charge whatever price you want for your products and services.

It is rumored that the Rolls Royce Ghost is built on the same chassis as the BMW 750. If this is true, that means the Ghost and the 750 are basically the same car. The BWM is $100,000 while the Rolls Royce is $300,000. Why? Well, let's take a look.

Both cars have four wheels, leather seats, power windows, power steering, and they would get you from point A to point B on about the same mileage. When we look at a car and consider what it's actually made for, we could even say that a Honda Civic has the same practical value as a BMW or a Rolls Royce. A Honda Civic also has four wheels, leather seats, power windows, power steering, and will get you from point A to point B.

At the end of the day, that's the purpose of a car: getting you from point A to point B.

You might argue that the Ghost has finer leather than the BMW or it has a few extra special features in it that the BMW doesn't have, but it can't be enough to justify a $200,000 difference in price. Here's the truth: the Rolls Royce Ghost justifies its huge price tag with its intrinsic value - its unseen value.

Imagine driving down the road in a BMW 750 and then driving down the same road in a Rolls Royce Ghost. Which car would get more attention from the people you drive by? The answer wouldn't surprise you; you're going to get way more heads turning in the Ghost.

There is a status upgrade associated with being in a Ghost. Having the experience of driving down the road and having people's heads turn, having people roll down their window and say, *"Hey! Sweet ride!"* - that's the intrinsic value that people pay for. The practical value - the utility - of the two cars might be the same, but the Ghost gives you more of an experience by elevating your status in society. The intrinsic value added to the Rolls Royce Ghost is why people are willing to pay $200,000 more.

That's the difference between practical value and intrinsic value. When designing your product or service, whether you have a brick-and-mortar business or you have an online business, you should think about what you can do to create intrinsic value around your brand.

Jonah Berger wrote a book called <u>Contagious</u>. It talks about an outrageously successful restaurant New York City named Crif Dogs that sells hotdogs. Crif Dogs is one of the most successful restaurants of all time. The restaurant is packed every single night and booked out months in advance. It's almost impossible to get a reservation to this place. How did Crif Dogs achieve such success?

Basically, they took a regular old hot dog and turned it into status symbol. And believe it or not, they don't do really any marketing either; it's all word of mouth.

One of the reasons people love the restaurant is its personality. In order to eat at Crif Dogs, you need to have a reservation. When you show up for dinner, there is a phone booth in the front part of the building. The phone booth contains an old rotary phone. You dial number 2 and some-one answers. The voice says, *"Do you have a reservation?"* If you don't have a reservation, you're not getting in. If you do, a secret door opens and you walk through to the actual restaurant. You feel like you're a part of some secret society or inner circle - not many people get to this point.

Literally every table is reserved every day! If you happen to be one of the lucky ones that secure a table, you now have bragging rights that you went and had a hotdog at Crif Dogs. At the end of the day, it's just a hotdog - but because of the intrinsic value added to it, it is one of the most successful restaurants in the city.

Berger also talks about a restaurant in Philadelphia that charges $100 for a cheesesteak. People can't wait to go eat this hundred dollar chees-esteak because of the intrinsic value around their brand. The status sur-rounding the restaurant compels people to pay 300%, 500%, and even 1000% more than what anybody else is charging - for the exact same thing.

Remember that as a business owner, people are not just going to purchase your product because of the practical value which you're giving them. They want that extra intrinsic value that they cannot get elsewhere. They want to feel special by purchasing your product. Your business needs to be distinct from others who are providing the same service as you are. Start thinking about what you can add to your business to make it stand out. If you can find something that adds real intrinsic value and you can communicate it to your audience, you'll watch your sales skyrocket.

Chapter 17
BAM!! You're Rich!!

"Never give in and never give up."
-Hubert Humphrey

Everyone wants to be rich. But what separates the rich from those who will never taste the success they dream of? It's the courage to get started and try something difficult even when you don't have everything figured out yet.

Over the years, I have met individuals who are willing to take that first dreaded step and have made a fortune due to their willingness to take that first step. Tyger Lucas from Houston, Texas is one individual I feel privileged to have come across. He has engaged in ventures even when he wasn't sure they would work out. To his great surprise, he found these ventures to be profitable. In fact, he made fortunes.

Before I met Tyger, Dr. Tabor Smith and I hosted a marketing summit called The GPS Summit. GPS stood for Growing Practice Strategies. The summit targeted chiropractors and we invited world renowned marketers within the chiropractic profession to speak. One of our guest speakers was Tyger Lucas. He gave the best talk of the entire event. Tyger shared his back story that explained how he generated tens of millions of dollars over the course of his career.

During the summit, Tyger talked about his triumphs and struggles in business. Here's an excerpt from his talk,

"And with all the positive motivation and all the positive stuff, good things started to happen. It wasn't easy. Success doesn't happen overnight, no matter what some people lead you to believe. The thing is there is no secret to success. It doesn't just happen. It was a struggle for me and one thing I learned along the way is, we all get kicked. The only

difference between successful people and unsuccessful people is, what do we do when we get kicked? Successful people just love getting kicked - that's another thing I've learned. I learned to love getting kicked because we're all gonna get kicked.

Trying to break through and make your millions isn't the easiest thing to do, but I have done it twice. The second time it happened, it came due to my persistence and my choice to walk in areas where others didn't want to. I kept on trying, never willing to give up. The success I got the second time around wasn't expected. When it happened; it happened suddenly. It was like stacking cherries on a wet paper towel. If you take a wet paper towel and start stacking cherries on it, the paper towel will eventually tear apart and the cherries will fall through, but you don't know which cherry is going to be the one to break the towel.

First you read one positive book. Then you go to a positive seminar. Then you learn something that makes you and your business better. Maybe you work on implementing it. Then you read another positive book and go to another positive seminar. Then you read another positive book. Then you go to another positive seminar. Then another positive book and another positive seminar. Then you read another positive book, then another, then another, then another, then another, and then BAM!! You're rich! And when it hits, it'll hit you so hard! Looking back you will see that the learning, hard work, consistency, and perseverance eventually pay off."

"*Bam! You're rich!*' became the catchphrase of the weekend. People were walking around the seminar and as they passed each other, they would point at each other and yell, □ *BAM!! You're rich!!*"

I went down to Houston a few years ago to see my friend Tabor. He invited Tyger to come out to lunch with us and Tyger shared the story of how he decided to start selling used cars on eBay. Actually, Tyger was one of the first people to sell cars on eBay.

Tyger would buy a used car for $2,000 and list it for $3,500. When he sold the car for $3,500, it gave him a profit of $1,500. He said he wasn't expecting to sell the car so easily. When it sold, he thought "*Holy crap, I just sold a car on the internet,! This is crazy!*" It raised his level of belief. He bought another car, listed it on eBay, and he sold that one, too. He kept on selling more and more cars!

Tyger told me there were times when he would buy a car, list it on eBay, and no one would buy it. If that happened, he would have to find other ways to move the car so he didn't lose money on it. This was a bit of a risk for him.

Tyger started going to dealerships that sold used cars and taking pictures of their cars. He'd upload the pictures to eBay. If the car on the lot was selling for $2,500, he would list it on eBay for $4,000 - and he didn't even own it! If the car sold on eBay, he would race down to the dealership praying to God that the car was still on the lot. If it was, he'd buy it and ship it to the customer. Eventually, he stopped selling cars he didn't actually own, but how genius is that?

In his early entrepreneurial days, Tyger took some big risks, but they turned out to be very beneficial. He ended up making millions of dollars selling cars on eBay. Tyger eventually took the money he earned and opened up a very high-end service center for luxury cars like Ferraris and Bentleys. He has a few locations now where they service high-end cars and he has gone on to make millions in that business, too.

If you haven't started your business yet because you don't have a product, you should apply Tyger's strategy. If you want to be an online marketer, your products would be things like online courses, e-books, video courses, live webinar events, summits, virtual summits, etc. Maybe you want to start, but you're "waiting" to create your product.

Here's what happens when you wait like that: you never end up creating the product. Next thing you know, six months, a year, 18 months, or 2 years have gone by and you're still "waiting" to create your product.

Don't wait. Follow Tyger's lead and host a webinar or put together a product launch. Dend out emails to people telling them about the course you are putting together as well as the benefits that they stand to gain from the course. You could tell them that in the future, the course will be sold for $997. Because the course isn't put together yet, they would be getting the product at a discounted price of $497.

Another friend of mine actually did this with a product he recently launched. He generated over $75,000 in sales and sold a product that he hadn't even created yet. Basically, he pulled a Tyger Lucas. He delivered the course to his buyers 4 weeks after they bought it. It also gave him motivation to get shit done.

You could do the exact same thing by putting together an online course and selling it at a discounted rate. It's a great way to just start generating revenue online and it will force you to go get that product done. One of the biggest challenges people have is procrastination. They think about what they ought to do that will generate money for them, but they don't actually do it.

If nothing is holding you accountable, then you're probably not going to do it. So why not sell a course now? Have those people that paid you hold you accountable to getting your shit done.

Chapter 18
Build a Massive Email List

Over the years, I have learned that every thousand people on your email list is the equivalent of six figures per year for your business.

When I first started online marketing in 2006, I sold my product that targeted chiropractors on eBay If you recall, it was the waiting room slide-show DVD called TICTalk. Each eBay sale gave me another person's email list. Selling lots of DVDs helped me gather tons of emails. At some point, I decided that I didn't want to sell only on eBay. So I had a website built, but I wasn't generating any new leads except from the ones I got from eBay.

I had a spreadsheet of emails which I wanted to utilize. That led me to buy a program called Mailloop, which I had to attach to my website server. After doing that, I started sending out emails and I started making sales through email marketing. I began to realize how important email marketing was, but the question still remained: how was I going to get more people on my email list?

I ended up buying an email list of chiropractors from a vendor. The list contained around 30,000 emails. I loaded them into Mailloop and sent my emails out. That was a HUGE MISTAKE. You see, none of those people opted into my list. None of them gave me permission to email them and wow, did I piss a bunch of people off. Also, because Mailloop was attached to my server, I ended up getting one of my websites shut down because of the spam complaints that came back from it.

Out of the 30,000 emails that were sent, only 80 emails were actually opened. Only 2 people clicked through. My attempt at using emails that I didn't earn myself failed spectacularly.

I didn't legitimately generate these subscribers, I purchased them. I'm bringing this up because some of you think buying email lists is a fast way to generate leads, but that is absolutely the wrong way to go about building an email list. You can get leads real fast by buying them, but I guarantee you you're going to piss a lot of people off and ruin your reputation. And it's not even effective, either.

I had a chiropractor friend of mine who made a post on social media about a company that offers a weight loss program. He didn't sign up for their email subscription, but they started spamming him. So what did he do? He went on social media and made it known who this company was and that they were sending spam to his inbox. Other people who had received the same emails commented on the post, complaining and tarnishing the name of the company.

But how do you actually generate an email list legitimately and turn that list into a six or even seven figure business?

First, you should create a freemium - a free offer. This should be something of immense value that you can give away for free in exchange for an email. People will provide you with their email address and opt in to get an eBook, mini-course or some sort of free report.

You should consider creating multiple freemiums based on different aspects of your business. For example, you could create an eBook or a short online course on how to upload videos to YouTube and SEO them. Another idea would be a free report on how to work with YouTube influencers to maximize their exposure. Maybe another free report on how to create killer YouTube videos that increase likes, comments, and subscribers would be viable.

If you teach Facebook marketing, you could explore creating a report or a mini-course on how to use Facebook Ads to generate leads online. You could also create a report on how to use Instagram Ads.

A good friend of mine was giving away a product which he sells for $149. The product is called Chiropractic Delivers and he gave it away in exchange for emails. On Facebook, he used paid traffic to target his specific audience. Inside the Facebook Ads Manager he specified that he wanted to target people that went to various chiropractic colleges. He knew that by targeting those colleges he was more than likely to tap into a large chiropractic population.

He told Facebook that he wanted to target anyone who had the job title of "chiropractor." Between the colleges and job title, his audience was about 80,000 people. He then ran ads for his freemium and generated thousands of leads, each of which gave him their email address.

Once people are on your email list, you'll want to nurture the list and builds relationships with the people on that list by providing additional value to them.

In 2009, I was thinking of how I was going to get more people on my email list. I created a free membership website called Chiropractic Secret Society where I put all kinds of content based around marketing and growing your practice using online and traditional marketing strategies.

Every week, I added valuable content to the website. Then I would email the people on my list and tell them that I had a website called Chiropractic Secret Society. I would give them the benefits of becoming a member and emphasize that membership to the site was free. I would provide a link to the landing page where they would opt-in with their name and email so they could get access to the content. In a few months, my email list grew from about 700 chiropractors to almost 2,000 through this strategy.

I continued to send emails out to the list every time I created a new training on how to improve SEO on YouTube, how to create a Google business listing, how to use social media to grow their practice, and all sorts of other trainings I had created.

I nurtured this list for a whole year and didn't sell anything to them - but I kept giving tons of free value to them. In 2010, I created a product called The Illuminati Internal Marketing System which consisted of 13 referral promotions that chiropractors could implement to increase new patient referrals.

I charged $597 for it and promoted it through a product launch. After a year of giving away free content to these people, I ended up doing $36,000 in sales from the launch initially. Sales kept coming in and over the next 12 months, I made another $100,000. That product also helped me promote other products. In that particular business, I made over $250,000 that year.

I was able to generate a quarter of a million dollars in 12 months from my email list of 2,000 people because I nurtured the list by providing immense value to them. The key to making six and seven figures online is to nurture your list and not make every email about selling stuff to them.

I use the 70-30 rule of email marketing. This rule guides my online marketing and sales operation. 70% of the time, I'm providing value to my list. 30% of the time, I sell to the people on my email list.

Here's another tip: Your competition probably only has one free offer - a report, an eBook, or a mini-course. I recommend making five, six, or seven free offers based on different aspects of your business. Use those multiple freemium offers to significantly increase your lead generation efforts.

I have a couple of friends who started a Posture Education Program for doctors. They have an email list of over 40,000 various healthcare professionals that they generated in 2 short years by creating multiple free offers. Their offers were things like: how to do an ergonomics talk for local businesses, the top 24 studies every healthcare professional needs to know about posture, how to become the official posture expert of a local sports team, and several other free reports. Having multiple lead magnets (freemiums) has paid off immensely for them. They have amassed over $3M in sales in 2 years.

In order to generate leads legitimately and quickly, you could do what's called a joint venture. This is where other marketers promote your information to help you generate leads. If they generate a lead and the lead turns into a sale, they can earn a commission. Commissions usually translate to 30%-50% of the sale.

For example, if you own a Facebook Ad Agency like me, you might approach someone in your niche that markets via Instagram and say, *"Hey look, I know you have a program on Instagram Ads, but I have got a program on Facebook Ads. If you send an email to your list about my program, I'll give you 40% of the sales and I can do the same for you."*

So if I have a $1,000 program and they send an email out to their list and drive traffic over to my funnel to opt in to get access to the freemium I'm offering and their leads turn into sales, I pay them a commission. But the key here is, the people coming from their list now opt-in to my email list. Then, I can continue to nurture a relationship with them. This is a really fast way to grow your list.

I have seen people go from having no one on their email list to having 3,500 people on their email list in a matter of days. Remember, don't look at people as being a competition - see them as allies!

Building your email list requires demonstrating creativity, giving value for free, and going out of your way to collaborate with other individuals who you know are specialists in other areas you might not be proficient in. Commence engaging in these strategies to grow your business and achieve that six or seven figure business you always dreamed of.

If you can apply the ideas and strategies discussed, you'll be able to position yourself as an expert and authority in your niche. Apply what you have learned and you will have created your own Propaganda Marketing Machine that is so big, and so badass at generating sales that you wouldn't even be able to turn it off if you wanted to.

P.S. If you enjoyed this book, I have a FREE Gift For You!

First open up your facebook messenger app and tap on the "home button" in the navigation bar at the bottom.

Next, tap on your profile picture in the upper left hand corner.

Third, tap on your personal messenger code.

Finally, tap on the Scan Code tab at the top of the app, hold your phone up and scan this code.

I'll send you a gift that will 10X your business in the next 12 months!

27597805R00063

Made in the USA
Lexington, KY
06 January 2019